Don't Eat That!

Force-Free Food Avoidance Training For

Dogs That Love To Scavenge

Predation Substitute Training – Volume 3

Simone Mueller

Co-Author Charlotte Garner
Illustrations Päivi Kokko

Don't Eat That! Force-free Food Avoidance Training for
Dogs that love to Scavenge has provided the most
accurate information possible. The techniques and
training protocols used in this manual are state-of-the-
art among science-based, force-free dog trainers and
behaviorists. The author shall not be held liable for any
damages resulting from use of this book.

Impressum:
Simone Mueller
Pattbergstrasse 15
74867 Neunkirchen
Germany

Simone Müller has done it again!

Another clearly written book full of eminently practical ways of resolving problematic scavenging behaviors in dogs!

She explores scavenging from multiple angles and suggests training processes and enjoyable games to redirect unsafe scavenging.

What I love most is how she respects the dog's needs, provides a rationale for them, and offers easy-to-implement and effective solutions while maximizing dogs agency and choice.

I highly recommend "Don't Eat That" for all those who live and/or work with dogs!

Risë VanFleet, PhD, RPT-S, CDBC, CAEBI
Author of The Human Half of Dog Training and Co-Author of Animal Assisted Play Therapy

Table of Contents

Introduction

Do you have to constantly scan the environment for discarded food to prevent your dog from eating it?

Are you embarrassed by your dog's scavenging behavior as you watch them disappear to raid someone's picnic?

Is it costing you a small fortune at the vets, after they have eaten something that has made them ill?

Are you tired of endlessly fishing something out of your dog's mouth and wondering what they have picked up this time?

Do you just wish you could enjoy a relaxed walk with your dog, without the fear of them constantly trying to scavenge?

Living with a dog who relentlessly scavenges food can be exhausting. So, it's completely understandable if it causes you significant amounts of stress, anxiety, and frustration.

And you are not alone!

Because scavenging is such a deep-rooted behavior for the vast majority of dogs, it can be exceptionally challenging to manage. This can result in owners choosing methods they may feel uncomfortable with, to try and change their dog's behavior and keep them safe.

But here is the good news!

Using the techniques and training protocol in this book can help you manage your dog's scavenging behavior in a kind yet effective way, with long-term results.

Instead of trying to eliminate your dog's scavenging entirely, the guidance here gives your dog a safe, suitable outlet for this completely natural behavior.

And for you, as their owner, you will finally feel relieved knowing that you have the tools to help your dog!

You will be able to say goodbye to stressful walks and no longer dread your dog picking something up which could be dangerous for them.

- You will understand why your dog loves to scavenge.
- You will find out how to get your dog to view you as part of the fun, instead of the one who always puts a stop to it, by providing them with more suitable outlets for their behavior.
- You will learn clever management techniques to prevent your dog from scavenging in the first place.
- You will become a master of exciting games that teach your dog to work with you instead of doing their own thing!
- You will be able to teach your dog how to let you know they have found something, instead of eating it straight away.
- You will know how to teach your dog emergency cues and when and how to use them in real life.
- Ultimately, you will be able to manage real-life scavenging scenarios effectively and safely, without any detriment to your dog.

You can achieve all this without using aversive training techniques and tools that can damage your relationship with your dog.

Stressful walks will become a thing of the past, and you will finally find relief knowing your dog is safe from eating something harmful to them.

This training protocol can be successful with any dog, regardless of their age, breed, or previous history. It's inclusive for everyone, no matter what your situation is!

If this all sounds too good to be true, believe me, it isn't! Once you start this training protocol, the only regret you will have is that you didn't know about it sooner!

So, let's get started!

How To Use This Book

Here is how you can achieve the best results with the information you will learn throughout the book:

Take One Step At A Time

This training protocol is broken up into small, achievable steps. This will help to set you and your dog up for success, instead of you feeling overwhelmed.

Although some steps may naturally be easier for your dog, please make sure you don't skip them. You should only proceed to the next step when at least 80% of your attempts are successful.

Mix Things Up A Little

It is a good idea to mix and match one game from each of the three sections; Management and Prevention, Core Games and Emergency Cues. This means you can always practice three games. This adds variety to your dog's training, so both you and your dog won't get bored or frustrated with working on the same thing continually.

Practice Regularly

Aim to practice each game for one to three minutes at a time, or for a maximum of ten repetitions in one session. You can repeat this once or twice a day.

Keep your training sessions short and sweet to keep your dog motivated and keen to learn more. Lengthy sessions are likely to be frustrating for your dog and they will be more inclined to make mistakes. So, even if they are doing well, it's better to end on a positive note instead of pushing too far and them getting it wrong.

Give Yourself A Break

It's best not to train for more than five days a week. Two days of the week should always be kept free for relaxation and fun activities! Although the training games in this protocol are fun, they still require a lot of concentration from your dog and you, so you both need a break!

If you or your dog had a bad day, take a break from training. We don't want frustration to kick in for you or your dog! If either of you are not in the right headspace to learn, your results won't be as good.

Play Scavenging Games Often

Holding back and NOT devouring food takes a lot of impulse control from your dog! It also builds frustration too so it's essential your dog has an outlet where they are allowed to scavenge. So, it's vital you give your dog regular scavenging opportunities by playing the Scavenging Games! This is one of the most important aspects of the whole protocol. Remember, we are not trying to eliminate scavenging from your dog's life entirely, we are aiming to let them practice it safely.

Consider Each Component

This training protocol is split into 4 main sections, Management & Prevention, Core Games, Scavenging Games and Emergency Cues. Each of these sections should be considered equally. If you only concentrate on one aspect of this, your results will not be as good. They are designed to work together as a whole, with each part complimenting and supporting each other.

DON'T EAT THAT

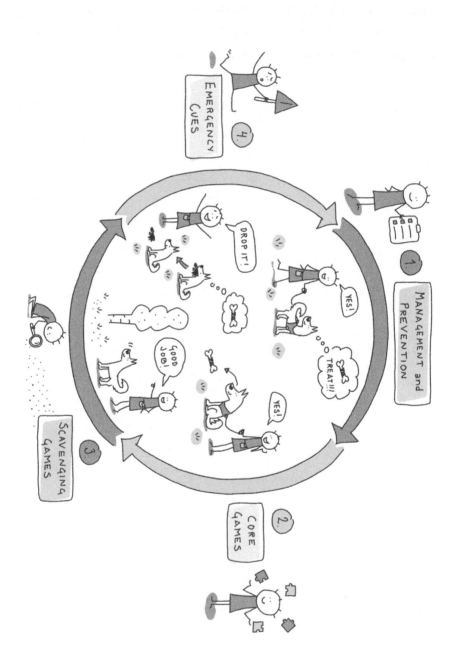

18

Think About Your Own Situation

The advice provided in this book is designed to be tailored to suit as many dogs as possible. However, certain parts of each exercise may not be suitable for your individual circumstances. For example, it's a good idea to only release your dog to the food on the ground intermittently to avoid your dog anticipating this being the next step. Also, if you are particularly traumatized by a previous incident where your dog scavenged something which made them very ill, then it's fine if you would prefer not to release your dog to the food they find on the ground as a bonus reward.

Finally, Have Fun!

Although the training protocol is important for managing your dog's scavenging successfully, it should never be done to the detriment of your dog. Training should be fun for both of you! And as soon as it isn't, take a break and do something else. Neither of you will learn anything if you both dread training together, so keep things upbeat!

And now: Have fun with your dog!

Download Your Free "Don't Eat That" Training Plan

To help you keep track of your training, I have designed a printable training diary to the Core Games that you can download from my website for free! Filling this in regularly will help you monitor your progress.

To download the training log, follow the link or scan the QR code:

https:// predation-substitute-training.com/ donteatthattraininglog

Which Methods Should I Avoid Using?

When you are faced with your dog being ruthlessly determined to scavenge anything they come across outside, you can understandably get quite desperate to stop this from happening. Not only is this kind of behavior frustrating for you as their owner, but it can also be quite dangerous for your dog. Eating rotten foods, livestock faeces, or discarded human food can be detrimental to your dog's health. So, it's essential you try and teach them not to grab everything they find on a walk!

It may be tempting for you to resort to aversive methods to try and stop your dog from scavenging as a matter of urgency. However, this isn't without its own problems. Here we will look at some reasons why some commonly recommended training methods and aversive tools can be much more trouble than they are worth:

Punishing Your Dog For Scavenging

A common suggestion is that you simply punish your dog for eating the food they found on the floor. Many owners' instinct is to shout, scream or even try to grab or hit their dog in an attempt to get them to drop their scavenged food. However, in reality, this will create one of three outcomes. First, it teaches your dog to swallow the food as quickly as they possibly can to avoid giving you the opportunity to take it from them. Or secondly, they could learn it's best to run rapidly away from you with their prize so they can gobble it down far away from you. Both of these results mean you simply have no chance to get the food off your dog, and either way, the food still gets consumed, which is exactly what we want to avoid! Thirdly, punishing your dog for stealing food from the floor can encourage them to become protective over the food. This is known as resource guarding, and it can cause even the usually most placid of dogs to show aggression towards you, so they get to keep hold of their newfound food.

Never Feeding Your Dog From The Ground

Another common suggestion to stop your dog from scavenging is to never feed your dog anything from the floor at all. Some trainers take this to the extreme and encourage you never to feed your dog from a bowl whatsoever. Instead, they encourage you to feed your dog their entire meal from your hand. While this may sound almost sensible, because it goes some way to teaching your dog that good things come from you, it's not likely to work in stopping them from scavenging. In reality, your dog will be unable to make the connection and generalize the scenarios of finding a pizza on the floor, with only receiving food from your hand. The truth is, they'll find it almost impossible to resist their newly discovered treasure. When faced with something delicious on the floor, your dog won't stop and think to themselves, 'oh, I best not eat that; I am not allowed to eat off the floor.' If only it were that simple! The temptation for them at that moment is just too great!

Muzzles

Muzzles should only be used as a short-term management solution, not as a long-term option to stop your dog from scavenging. The only type of muzzle that would prevent your dog from eating discarded food is an 'occlusion muzzle.' These prevent your dog from opening their mouth completely, thereby stopping them from being able to grab and eat food from the ground. However, in the process, it also prevents your dog from being able to pant freely or drink, which can be life-threatening. Dogs should never be exercised whatsoever when wearing an occlusion muzzle; they're strictly designed to be worn for a few moments at a time. For example, while your vet gives your dog an injection, then, the muzzle should be removed to allow your dog to breathe freely. Occlusion muzzles can cause your dog a great deal of discomfort and suffering if used incorrectly, so you should always avoid them for instances like this. Even if you fit your dog with a basket muzzle, which allows them to pant freely, it still allows them to scavenge. Granted, they would be unable to eat larger pieces of discarded food, but they can still shove their muzzle into food and lick it off the inside, which is still rewarding for a dog who wants to scavenge! We need to try and change how your dog responds and feels about finding discarded food instead of just limiting how much of it they can consume. Wearing a muzzle doesn't teach your dog not to scavenge; it will just frustrate them being unable to do it.

Rank Reductions

Some suggest that your dog is scavenging when they're out and about because they don't respect you, and you need to show them you're in charge. Even if this were to be the case, the likelihood of your dog making a connection between these methods and not eating something tasty from the ground is pretty much impossible! Advice on how to show your dog who's boss includes; making sure you always eat before your dog, not letting them onto your sofa, not allowing them to sleep in your bed, walking through doorways before them, taking their food off them when they're eating, and 'alpha rolling' them onto their side or back to prove you're the alpha or boss.

Rank reduction techniques such as this are advised on the basis that we live in a pack hierarchy with our dogs, which has since been scientifically proven to be inaccurate. In fact, the very scientist who first discovered and promoted the idea that our dogs see us as part of their pack, as wolves would, has since withdrawn this way of thinking. Further studies have since proved that the study Professor. L. David Mech refers to in his 1970's book 'The Wolf - The Ecology and Behavior of an Endangered Species' was highly flawed. The study researched captive wolves' behavior and social hierarchy and applied the findings to our domesticated dogs. However, the dynamic of a group of wild wolves is exceptionally different from those in captivity and different again from the dogs we share our lives with today. In the wild, wolves tend to live in a family group, all related in some way, and they don't have an 'alpha' male or female as once was thought. Instead, they have a pair of wolves who breed, while the rest help care for the cubs when they are born. They resolve conflicts peacefully and only use fighting and aggression as a last resort. This is actually much more like our domesticated dogs today, who often go out of their way to avoid conflict or uncomfortable situations. We now know that the notion of our dogs trying to be 'dominant' or 'alpha' or 'pack leader' over us is entirely untrue. Nor will they see us in those roles, simply because we are not wolves, our dogs are not wolves, and we don't live in a pack together. We are just two species who are doing the best we can to understand one another.

Punishing The Food

Punishing the food is as bizarre as it sounds, although it's still relatively commonly recommended non the less. Some trainers suggest that you behave aggressively towards the food on the floor to discourage your dog from approaching it. Not only will you look completely mad hitting a pizza, or shouting at a sandwich on the floor, but it's also improbable to teach your dog not to eat it! Depending on your dog's personality, this advice can cause two different outcomes. Nervous, uncertain dogs can become easily scared by you suddenly behaving so aggressively. Because you are a role model for your dog, it can cause them to lose trust in you if they see you behaving violently or erratically, even if you're not directing it at the dog themselves. Or, if your dog is quite confident or excitable, they can see this as a game and try to join in by grabbing the food or simply wait until you're finished and rush in to grab it anyway!

Aversive Tools

Some owners will often consider resorting to using aversive tools like shock collars, (also known as e-collars), prong collars, choke chains, pet corrector sprays, water sprays, or shaker bottles in a desperate bid to stop their dog from scavenging. And unfortunately, you are likely to get the desired results using these methods. However, not without severely damaging the relationship between you and your dog, sometimes irreparably. These are the most unethical option available to you, and the risk of fallout from inaccurate timing is high. To use these types of aversives, you need impeccable timing and accuracy. Without this, you're likely going to be causing pain to your dog in relation to something else instead of when they go to pick up food from the floor. For example, you activate the shock collar when you think your dog's about to pick up some discarded food, but it happens when they're looking at a child nearby. This forms a negative association with the child, not the food as you intended. This can cause your dog to show aggression towards a child in the future, as they associate that with the pain they felt when they saw them. In line with the 'LIMA' protocol, which stands for 'Least Intrusive, Minimally Aversive,' tools such as this have no place in ethical, kind dog training. When you consider that you can achieve your desired results using the kind training exercises provided in this book, I would question why you would knowingly inflict pain, discomfort, and fear onto your dog when it's not at all necessary.

Why Do Dogs Love To Scavenge?

The fact you are reading this book means there is a high chance that you already know that dogs love to scavenge! But you might be surprised to learn that there are several deep-rooted reasons for this; it's not as simple as them just feeling hungry or being greedy! Understanding why your dog loves scavenging so much can help you better work out how to manage this behavior successfully.

So, here are the reasons why your dog values scavenging so highly:

Scavenging Is A Basic Need For Your Dog

Something that every species of living beings rely upon is finding food. This is essential to their survival and is no different for our dogs. Although our domesticated pet dogs no longer rely on scavenging as their only way of finding food, it is often still something they naturally desire and feel the need to do.

Your Dog Is Simply Hungry

This is perhaps the most common reason which comes to mind when owners are faced with a scavenging dog! Many think their dog is doing it to be greedy, but in actual fact, they may be hungry. Some modern-day dog foods don't satisfy your dog's hunger for long, so when they come across something tasty on the ground, it can be tough for them to resist, even if it's something potentially harmful to them. Consider the type and amount of food your dog is getting, and how often they are fed over the day. Making changes to these things can be a good starting point for reducing your dog's scavenging, although it won't eliminate it completely! Even dogs who are fed high-quality foods can still find the temptation of some 'freebies' too difficult to ignore! Try feeding your dog a handful of food around 20 minutes before you go for a walk. Do this for a week and see if this can reduce their scavenging urges.

Dogs Find Scavenging Intrinsically Reinforcing

There are two things at play here that make scavenging intrinsically reinforcing for our dogs - their seeking and play systems. The seeking system is the most addictive of the two and can be likened to people who enjoy gambling. Although they don't win every time they take part, the thrill of the possibility of winning keeps them coming back for more again and again. They invest increasing amounts of time, energy, and concentration in anticipation of a win that might happen, in exactly the same way a human would when playing on slot machines or placing bets. When your dog wins by finding something to eat on the floor, the feeling of euphoria and excitement, along with the Dopamine that is released into their system, makes them want to scavenge again.

The play system means that scavenging feels good for your dog, they enjoy it, and it makes them happy! Your dog's enjoying the searching, finding, sniffing, chewing, licking, eating, and swallowing aspects of scavenging food. This releases feel-good endorphins into your dog's system, leaving them happy, satisfied, and relaxed. It's not hard to see why they would want to repeat this process as often as possible so that they can feel this way more often! This is similar to how humans feel when we have a lavish 3-course meal. We feel indulged and will look forward to the next opportunity we have to experience this.

Scavenging Is Genetically Anchored Into Your Dog

Wolves first started spending time closer to humans because they realized there was food near them that was easily accessible. Humans created waste and stored food, which was much easier for the wolves to scavenge from than trying to hunt and kill their own food. This relationship turned out to be mutually beneficial as the wolves deterred other animals and intruders from getting too close to the humans. This sparked the start of evolution from wolves to the dogs we know and love today.

Some wild dogs still live in a very similar way to their ancestors, living on the outskirts of villages and scavenging from what the villagers leave behind. Some breeds still retain these strong instincts to scavenge, even though they no longer depend on it for their survival.

Your Dog Is Used To Needing To Scavenge

The saying 'old habits die hard' is relevant to dogs who have been used to needing to scavenge to survive. Dogs that have lived on the streets, often for several months, need to scavenge food to eat. This could be hunting and killing animals, or the easier route for them is scavenging food that humans leave behind. In fact, their whole life will have been structured around finding food, and it will have taken up a large part of each day for them. They will have practised their scavenging skills to make them excellent at finding things to eat, so they are not wasting precious time and energy searching for food. So, it can be tough for them to stop suddenly, even if their new lifestyle no longer requires them to do it.

Boredom Can Make Your Dog Scavenge More

This is particularly common in breeds with high intelligence and energy levels. If they're not provided with enough mental and physical stimulation, your dog may start using scavenging to remedy their boredom. This gives them something fun and rewarding to do. So, it's important to ensure your dog's mental and physical needs are met, before you start this training protocol. Without this, the training won't be as effective.

Over-aroused Dogs Tend To Scavenge More

Dogs that are stressed, anxious, or over-aroused can use scavenging as a way to distract themselves and make themselves feel better. Dogs that are reactive towards other animals, people, and new scenarios can be more likely to resort to scavenging to try and help them feel more in control and calmer. If you think that your dog is scavenging because of underlying stress, or to try and distract themselves from stressful situations, it's best to contact a force-free trainer or behaviorist for advice prior to starting this training protocol.

Your Dog Is Searching For A Novel Taste

Humans tend to be creatures of habit, and we like to stick with what we know. So often, once we find a food that suits our dog, we stick with the same flavor, day after day, month after month. Although this might be the most convenient option for us, it is by far the most boring option for our dogs! Unless they suffer from allergies or intolerances, our dogs can benefit from having a wide selection of different flavors and protein sources in their diet. Whether they are raw fed, kibble fed, or you cook at home for them, so long as their diets are complete, nutritious, and tasty for them, that is the main thing! It will quickly become monotonous if dogs constantly eat the same food for extended periods. This can lead to them having a stronger urge to scavenge in a desperate bid to find something different and more exciting to eat!

Artificial Selection Can Increase Scavenging

The artificial selection of certain breeds can increase the likelihood and frequency of their scavenging behavior. This is regularly shown in members of the hound family, who are bred to live and work in large packs of other hounds. Many working hounds live in a large group and are fed together, meaning it's in their best interest to find, grab and eat the food as quickly as possible, to make sure they get a decent amount. Those that are not as fast, will get little to no food and will be hungry, so it's beneficial for them to refine their scavenging skills to become more successful at it.

Also, some gundog breeds like the Labrador, Flat Coated Retriever, and Golden Retriever have been found to be missing part of or all of the gene known as POMC. The Proopiomelanocortin gene (POMC) gene affects appetite, food motivation, fat storage, and, most importantly, satiety. Satiety signals when your dog is full; without this signal working correctly, which is the case with dogs with the faulty POMC gene, they won't know that they feel full. So, they will continue to eat more, even though they have had enough! This can understandably increase their scavenging, as they constantly feel hungry, even if they are well-fed and nourished.

Your Dog May Have A Medical Condition

If your dog is an excessive scavenger, or has recently started scavenging much more than usual, it is best to get them checked thoroughly by your vet to rule out any potential medical issues before you begin training. If your dog's scavenging is due to a medical condition, then this training protocol won't be successful until your dog has received the appropriate treatment to cure or manage their condition effectively. Conditions like gastroenteritis, gastritis, heartburn, indigestion, pancreatitis, acid reflux, IBD, and parasites can all increase scavenging because your dog is looking for something to make themselves feel more comfortable or to ease their symptoms.

Pica Makes Your Dog Need To Scavenge

Pica is a disorder that makes your dog crave and eat non-food substances. This can mean pebbles, wood, plastic, paper, or anything else that is non-nutritional, wouldn't be considered as food, and holds no physical value to your dog. It is not fully understood what causes

Pica. Some say it is a medical condition, related to stress and anxiety, because of boredom, or a habit the dog has formed. Whatever the reasoning behind the Pica, you should work with a qualified behaviorist under the advice of your veterinarian to try and manage it effectively before beginning this training protocol.

What Are Scavenging Games, And How Can They Help?

Now that you better understand why your dog wants to scavenge so much, it's time to look at more suitable ways to provide them with an outlet for this need. This is where scavenging games are invaluable! They allow your dog to scavenge in a safe, manageable environment that gives them the chance to practice something they enjoy and value without the risk of them being in danger.

We now know that scavenging is a deep-rooted, intrinsic need for our dogs, and this is not something we can stop completely; the desire and urge for them to do it will always be there. So, instead of trying to eliminate scavenging behavior entirely, you will see more sustainable results if you give your dog an outlet that mimics a real-life scenario.

Here are some suggestions of games to give your dog the scavenging experience they crave in a fun and exciting way, while still maintaining a controlled environment:

Scavenging Islands

Scavenging islands work on the basis that your dog is always allowed to scavenge in a designated spot. This replicates when stray and feral dogs will often hang around the same location each day, as they know there is likely to be food for them to scavenge. So, choose a spot out on your walk or in your garden. Wherever you choose, ensure this spot is always the same and available for scavenging. This creates predictability for your dog, which in turn, encourages calmness and relaxation. This will also help form a habit and routine for your dog, who will soon recognize that they are always allowed to scavenge in this particular place. Dogs are extremely capable of learning that they are only allowed to practice certain behaviors in a specific location, which is what we are trying to achieve here. When they get the opportunity to practice scavenging regularly in a designated area, it can reduce the likelihood of them trying to do it elsewhere.

Treasure Hunts

To create a treasure hunt, sprinkle tiny pieces of food over the ground for your dog to sniff out and find. This works exceptionally well in grassy areas as your dog will rely on their sense of smell to find the treats instead of being able to see them first. Choosing treats with a residual scent like flakes of tuna, strong grated cheese, chopped liver, etc., can create more interest for your dog, as they will leave a scent behind even after your dog has eaten the treats. This is a better choice than kibble or other dried biscuits, which are easily visible to your dog and don't leave a smell behind after they have been eaten. The sniffing, licking, and chewing parts of this process will tire your dog out mentally and allow them to practice scavenging safely.

Dissecting Wrapped Foods

This game mimics the dissecting part of the scavenging process. Try wrapping up tasty treats, a small amount of human food, or a chew. Try using some wrapping paper, kitchen towel, a toilet roll holder, a cardboard box, baking parchment paper, etc., and let your dog shred and rip it open to access the treats. It shouldn't be an issue if your dog consumes any small parts of the wrapping material. But, if they are consuming it in large quantities, try wrapping the food in a large cabbage or lettuce leaf instead. Then this way, it doesn't matter if they eat the wrapping too!

Taste Mimicking

Some dogs crave the taste of poop, rotten foods, or rubbish. All of these items have strong, distinctive smells and tastes. So, while they cannot consume the actual items, you can try and mimic them for your dog. Here are some options for you to try:

- Sauerkraut (or other fermented foods available to you that are safe for your dog to eat)
- Stinky cheeses
- Red smear-ripened cheeses (the red rind is created by the smear bacteria and creates the strong smell)
- Tripe (cow or sheep stomach)
- Rumen (first stomach of a cow)
- Omasum (third stomach of a cow).

Although these options might not sound very appealing to us, chances are your dog will love them! And they are the closest mimic to the things your dog craves the most.

Novel Food Platters

Some dogs scavenge because they are desperately seeking novel and interesting tastes. So, if you create tasting platters for them, this can help them experience new flavors and scents in a safely managed way. Don't mix all the different foods; keep them separate so your dog can choose exactly which ones they want to try. Consider different textures, flavors, scents, types of food, etc., so your dog has a broad range of new things to try. Be warned; it will probably get messy! So, it's best to do this outside or on an easily cleaned floor of your house. Do this regularly and be creative! Think of it as a grazing platter for your dog. It doesn't matter if they eat all of the items, only some of them, or even none of them; it is all about your dog experiencing them.

Don't give up too early with new foods! Even if your dog doesn't seem interested in something the first time they come across it, continue to offer it again in the future. Just like humans, our dog's tastes and preferences can change over time. So, sometimes your dog needs to be exposed to something new several times until they decide to try it!

Human Food For Dogs

Occasionally offer your dog foods designed specifically for human tastes like burgers, hotdogs, kebabs, pizza, sandwiches, fish and chips, etc. The general rule here is that if you could feed it to a 3-year-old human child, it is acceptable to feed it to your healthy dog in small quantities. Try occasionally hiding these food items on your scavenging island or offering them on your food platters so your dog can experience them. You can also use them regularly as your super treats for training. This way, your dog may be less likely to crave these things if they already have access to them anyway! Always check with your vet if you are unsure whether your dog can eat a particular food. And remember, human food should only make up a very small percentage of your dog's daily calorie intake, and they shouldn't be fed these things exclusively.

Tasty Table Scraps

Although some trainers still advise never to feed your dog from the table, there is actually nothing wrong with giving your dog human food leftovers. Provided that it is safe for your dog to eat, then it's fine to feed your dog table scraps each day. In fact, before commercial dog food was so readily available, all domestic dogs were fed leftovers from whatever their humans were eating that day. Obviously, this should be done in moderation, too, so don't give them half a pizza just because it's left over, but a small piece of pizza crust would be fine! Always make sure you use common sense, and if you are not sure it's safe for your dog, then it's best to avoid giving it to them.

Snuffle Mats And Slow Feeders

There are loads of different options available to purchase online or in pet stores, but you can also make your own too. Simply sprinkle small treats over a large bed sheet, towel, or blanket, and fold it, so your dog has to snuffle and move the fabric around to access the treats. There are also lickmats, kongs, and other food toys to consider using too.

Many owners simply see slow feeders as a way of slowing their dog down when they're eating. However, they can also be used more creatively by smearing wet or spreadable foods over them to encourage your dog to lick and move their mouth and tongue in different directions. This is more challenging and enriching for them than just picking their kibble out of them.

A Warning About Enrichment Toys

Enrichment toys, puzzle toys, slow feeders, and food toys can be a blessing or a curse, depending on how you use them. While they are great for creating a challenge for your dog that is more enriching for them to solve than simply eating from a bowl, they can also be highly frustrating. So, only use them in moderation. Your dog should not be fed solely from enrichment toys, as this

Simone Mueller

will be very frustrating for them! Especially if you increase the difficulty each time your dog tries to solve the puzzle.

Enrichment is designed to be a challenge for your dog's brain and/or body, so the idea of them having to do this before every bit of food they eat is unfair. Imagine you are in a restaurant waiting for your food to arrive, you are really hungry and can't wait to eat your meal. The waiter brings your food to you, puts it in front of you, and then sets you the challenge of solving a complex math problem before you are allowed to eat. How annoying and frustrating would this be for you?

This is not the aim of enrichment. The objective is to add happiness and fulfillment to your dog's life, not stress and frustration!

What Will I Need To Start Training?

Before you start training your dog to ignore discarded food or poop when they're out on walks, there are a few things you'll need to get to prepare yourself first. Make sure you have all of the following to hand before you begin:

- Marker Cue or Clicker
- Excellent Reinforcers (Ranging from so-so treats up to super treats!)
- Training Diary
- Short Leash and Long Leash
- Treat Pouch
- Toys
- Lidded Tubs
- Muzzle

The main thing to remember before training commences is that you need to be prepared to train your dog over a period of time consistently. Overcoming scavenging ethically isn't something that happens in one training session, so you need to stay committed. Remember, the temptation your dog is facing is enormous! Every part of them wants to grab that pizza, horse poop, or any other discarded food, so it's going to take some convincing that what you have to offer them is the best alternative.

Also, dogs that have already successfully scavenged food from the floor regularly have reinforced this behavior. They grab the food and eat it, which is exactly what they want to do. The more they are allowed to practice this, the more they'll want to do it again and again! Coupled with this reinforcement, your dog will also have learned by now that you are a big 'party-pooper' who only wants to steal their treasure and stop their fun! Changing your dog's perception of you is a huge part of overcoming their scavenging and stealing of food.

Be prepared to adjust the training to better suit your own dog. While some dogs will breeze through this training process, others may need smaller steps to help them be successful. It's crucial you don't get frustrated or try and rush through the steps, as this is more likely to set your dog up for failure instead of success, which is not something we want. Even if you are confident that your dog can successfully complete a particular step, it's best to still work through it anyway to really cement their learning. Avoid skipping steps as you are better off training each stage a little too much instead of not enough and letting your dog make mistakes.

Now we will look at each item in more detail and explore why they will be helpful to your training:

Marker Cue or Clicker

A marker is a predictable word or noise used to tell the dog they have done something right! Some people use this in place of a clicker, but the basis of how they are used and how they work is the same. Usually 'Yes' or 'Good.' It is used to mark the exact moment that your dog is showing a behavior that you would like to reward and see more of. A marker does not get your dog to do anything, it simply lets them know this behavior is going to be rewarded.

Some owners find it easier to use a clicker to mark the exact moment your dog shows desirable behavior. This increases accuracy, reduces timing errors, and creates the same noise each time, so your dog fully understands what it means. However, it can be a bit of a juggle holding your dog's lead, a clicker, treats, etc., so you may find it less cumbersome to use a marker cue instead. Provided you use the same marker cue every time (e.g., 'Yes' or 'Good') and your timing is accurate, then it can be equally as effective as using a clicker. Whichever you choose to use, it's simply there to mark the moment you want, and you should always follow it up immediately with a reward of food, play, praise or environmental (like letting your dog swim for example.)

Excellent Reinforcers

This is perhaps the most essential part of the process. You need to find out exactly what motivates your dog and use this as a high-value reward to reinforce behavior. Pairing training with fantastic rewards increases effectiveness and keeps your dog eager to learn more. It's a good idea to create a list of the things your dog finds more rewarding. Number them from 1 to 10, with 10 being something your dog likes but doesn't go wild over (so-so treats), all the way up to number 1, which is what they go crazy for (super treats)! It's a good idea to think outside the box here and choose things your dog doesn't usually have access to. The whole reason that teaching your dog not to scavenge can be difficult is that they value the sandwich or chips much more than whatever we are offering them. If we can find something that's of higher value to our dog than the discarded food, then we are onto a winner!

If your dog wants to pick up poop, you may wish to use a strong-smelling cheese as a reward for not eating it. This provides your dog with a scent that is similar to poop, which will be enticing and interesting for them. If you have a dog who loves to steal sandwiches from the ground, you could use small parts of a sandwich as a reward for choosing yours instead of the discarded one. Always ensure that the rewards are interesting and highly valuable to your dog! The aim here is to find a reward that is as close as possible to the thing your dog wants to scavenge from the ground. Of course, we can't offer them anything rotten or dangerous for them, but it needs to be of equal or higher value to them, or else they will simply choose to scavenge the food anyway. If your dog loves to eat human food they find on the floor, it's a good idea to mimic that by rewarding them with meatballs, burgers, pizza, tinned sardines, roast meats, hotdog sausages, etc. While these foods may not be nutritionally valuable to your dog, in the quantities we will be using for training purposes, they will be safe for them. And most importantly, they'll be more appealing to them than standard dog treats you can buy at the supermarket.

If your dog prefers to be rewarded with a toy instead of food, that's okay too! Use a toy that can have food rewards stuffed inside it. This lets your dog play with it, as well as receive a tasty treat from it too. Win, win!

Training Diary

It's advisable for you to start keeping a diary of your training. This allows you to monitor your progress and also makes sure you are staying on the right track. Outline the training games you will be working through (we will cover these later in the book), and then you can tick them off as you progress through them. In the diary, you can also make a note of the cues you have chosen to use so that the same ones are used consistently throughout the process. This also enables anyone else actively involved in your dog's care and training to know and understand exactly what's being taught to them. Consistency and repetition are the keys to successfully overcoming your dog's scavenging, and a training diary can help you with this.

Short Leash and Long Leash

Your short leash should be around 2.5 meters (98.5 inches) long, and your long leash should be between 10-15 meters or (395-590 inches) in length. You will be using both at different stages of the training process, depending on the activity you're doing and the environment you are in. Long leashes should always be attached to a well-fitting harness instead of a collar. This reduces the risk of damaging your dog's delicate neck if they pull or stop suddenly.

Treat Pouch

This should ideally be attached to your waistband or fastened securely around your waist. Your dog shouldn't be able to access the treats from the pouch directly, so one with a closeable top is recommended to stop them from being a pickpocket or thief! This also prevents the treats from falling out if you bend down too. However, the treats need to be easily accessible, so you can reward your dog quickly after using your clicker or marker cue. So, don't choose one that's too complicated, or takes ages to get the treat out for your dog. Some owners prefer silicone treat pouches as you can easily wash them, which is a must if you use strong-smelling food rewards!

Toys

If your dog is more motivated by toys than treats, you'll need a good selection of toys to use as rewards. You can rank the toys in order of appeal as we did with the treat rewards. So, even if a tennis ball is your dog's favorite thing at home, it doesn't necessarily mean they'll still choose that over a pizza on the floor when out on a walk! So, it has to be super rewarding and exciting for them. You could also use toys that can have food put inside them to double your dog's jackpot. Toys with pouches in like gundog dummies can be useful for this. They contain a secure pouch section to add treats to. Then your dog can play with the toy as a reward and get the chance to eat from it too! Double the fun and motivation!

Lidded Tubs

Plastic tubs with lids are helpful for allowing your dog to smell the food without them having direct access to it. You can then carefully pierce holes in the top to allow more of the food's scent to escape. Of course, a clever dog may realize they can pick up the whole tub and break into it to steal the food, but this is something we will work on! You could also use a bird fat ball holder, a fish grilling basket, or even a small animal trap cage. These items will be used in the same way as the lidded tubs once your dog has progressed further along their training journey.

Muzzle

A muzzle is more of a management tool than a long-term solution. However, getting your dog used to wearing one and feeling comfortable is still a good idea. They can be a handy training tool, particularly during the early stages of your training. Make sure your dog can pant and drink freely when wearing their muzzle. If they can't, walking or exercising your dog is extremely dangerous as they have no way of cooling themselves down.

For this reason, you need a well-fitting basket-style muzzle. The brand and size will vary depending on your dog's face and snout shape, so you may need to try a few different ones to get the best fit for them. You could get one custom-made for your dog's measurements if you prefer.

Training Tools

Super-Treat Ideas

Container ideas: live trap for mice, roasting tray for fish, fat ball feeder for wild birds

Basic Exercises for Management and Prevention

We now know that it's an unrealistic expectation to eliminate your dog's desire to scavenge completely. So, it's important you know how to effectively manage it to keep your dog safe. Management and prevention is even more crucial when you are just starting out on your force-free food avoidance training because your dog is much more likely to still be scavenging uncontrollably at this point. Although, even after you have worked through the entire training protocol, management and prevention will still play a vital role in your dog's day-to-day life. So, next up, we will look at several different management techniques that can be helpful for your dog right the way through your training:

Feeding Times

If your dog is constantly scavenging, it could potentially be because they are hungry. This is often overlooked in favor of more complex reasons, but it could simply be because of hunger. It's always worth considering hunger first before investigating other potential causes, which can require much more training and time to overcome.

Scavenging because of hunger can be easily managed effectively by looking at the times your dog is fed over the day in relation to the time they are exercised.

So, for example, if your dog is only getting one meal per day in the evening, but they go for their walk before this evening meal, you may find their scavenging is more intense. This is because they have gone for almost a full 24 hours without food, which is not a healthy way to feed your dog. Long periods of fasting can cause your dog's blood glucose levels to be unstable and erratic, which often has a negative impact on other behavioral issues, as well as increasing their need to scavenge.

Instead, try splitting their daily meal into two portions, one for the morning and one for the evening. This should leave your dog feeling more satisfied and less likely to want to scavenge food from the floor on walks, because they are simply not as hungry as they were before. Even if your dog is not a huge scavenger, it is still advisable to split their meals into at least two daily portions instead of one large meal.

However, for some dogs, simply splitting their meal into two or three daily portions will not completely stop them from wanting to pick up food on walks. This is especially common in high-energy working breeds, who often burn off their calories much faster than more sedate dogs, who take things at a slightly slower pace. For more intense dogs like this, try feeding them 1 hour before their exercise. This gives them time to digest their food before any strenuous activity, but not enough time for their blood glucose levels to dip, leaving them feeling hungry again once more.

Another top tip is to try feeding your dog a small amount of carbohydrates (approximately the size of your palm) right before they go for their walk. This too can help keep their blood glucose levels stable. This technique has also been seen to aid other issues for reactive dogs or those desperate to chase and hunt. While this tip won't stop these behaviors from happening entirely, it can help put your dog in a better frame of mind for listening and learning successfully.

You could also try adding more carbohydrates to your dog's meal. Brown rice, wholemeal pasta, oats, or boiled potatoes are great ways to fill up your dog and keep them feeling more satisfied and less hungry. In the same way, we can be less likely to pick up snacks or junk food if we eat 3 balanced, healthy meals per day; your dog will be less likely to scavenge for food if they feel full and well nourished. These extra carbohydrates should be healthy for your dog to eat and simple for them to digest. Try to avoid processed refined carbohydrate products like white bread, pizza dough, pastry, or chips. Although these are a source of carbohydrates, they are also highly processed and are likely to contain high levels of fat and sugar too, which is bad news for your dog's waistline if they are eating them regularly!

Muzzle Training

Your dog wearing a muzzle is a management tool that you should only use while you're working on stopping them from scavenging. As we have previously mentioned, it is not a long-term option or a substitute for proper training. Simply putting a muzzle on your dog doesn't teach them not to scavenge; it is only a management technique. However, muzzles do have their place in this process and can be particularly useful if you are walking in high-risk areas. Examples could include fields containing crops that have recently been sprayed with chemicals, places where there have been previous incidents of poisoned bait, or areas where you know there is likely to be discarded food. If it's not possible for you to avoid these areas entirely, a muzzle gives you an extra layer of security when your dog is there with you.

Aside from the scavenging aspect, teaching your dog to wear a muzzle is a valuable life skill for them to develop. It's likely that they may find themselves in a situation where they need to wear a muzzle at some point in their life. This could be if they, unfortunately, had an accident and needed emergency veterinary care or even for routine veterinary treatment. For many vet practices, it's common protocol to muzzle a dog for staff safety, particularly in emergencies where the dog's behavior can be unpredictable and erratic. These high-stress situations can be made marginally less stressful for your dog if they are already used to wearing a muzzle.

However, it's not as simple as just grabbing your dog and putting a muzzle on them! They need to be introduced and trained to wear a muzzle properly to ensure they feel comfortable in them. The main aim of this game is to encourage your dog to willingly put their snout into a muzzle before working up to fastening the straps and letting them wear it properly. By the end of this training game, your dog's muzzle should be like us humans wearing glasses - no big deal!

What You Will Need:
- Ice cream tub, yoghurt pot, jars, etc
- Basket-style muzzle
- Super treats
- Spreadable treats like cream cheese, cheese spread, pate, liver paste, doggy-safe peanut butter, etc.

The Aim Of The Game:

- To get your dog to willing put their snout into a muzzle
- To get your dog to feel comfortable wearing a muzzle

NOTE:

If your dog shows any sign of stress, anxiety, or discomfort during the muzzle training process, it's likely you have progressed too quickly. As with any training, it's essential you go at a pace that suits your dog. If they appear uncomfortable at any point, go back a step and make sure they are certain about things before moving on. Some dogs may breeze through this game in a matter of days, whereas others may take much longer. However long it takes, this game will be worth it, in the long run, to help your dog feel entirely comfortable wearing a muzzle.

Step 1

Start by encouraging your dog to put their full snout into a yoghurt pot, ice cream tub, or jar (depending on the size of your dog!), and let them lick some spreadable treats from the bottom of the pot. This gets them used to the feeling of having their whole snout inside an enclosed area. Don't force your dog to put their nose into it; they should willingly choose to do so.

Repeat this step regularly until your dog feels comfortable choosing to put their whole snout into the tub or pot.

Step 2

Once your dog is comfortable with the tubs or jars, you can repeat this process with the muzzle. Spread some spreadable treats onto the inside of the muzzle and hold it in your hand at your dog's level. Encourage your dog to put their snout in and lick the treats. Keep the muzzle and your hand still, as this allows your dog to choose to move towards it. Never move the muzzle towards your dog's face, as this can be enough to put a more sensitive dog off learning. Again, they shouldn't be forced into it; it should be their choice to approach it.

Repeat this step until your dog willingly chooses to put their snout into the muzzle. Don't worry if they only remain there for a few seconds; you can build up the duration over time.

Step 3

Once your dog is comfortable having their whole snout in the muzzle for a good few moments, loosely fasten the strap so you can still remove it quickly if they become overwhelmed. Feed them super treats through the front of the muzzle to help form a positive association.

Repeat this step frequently in short training sessions over several days.

Step 4

Once you have reached this step, it should be possible to fasten the muzzle's straps properly. Again, feed some super treats to make sure your dog feels confident and happy wearing it. You can then begin to gradually build up the duration of the time your dog wears the muzzle.

NOTE:

Never grab your dog and put the muzzle on them without proper training. This will scare them, make them panic, and undo any progress you have made with your muzzle training so far. They will see the muzzle as something to be afraid of, which is exactly what we don't want for them! We need to help our dogs to see that wearing a muzzle is something positive and nothing stressful for them.

Forming Positive Associations With Your Dog's Bowl

Although this might sound unusual, how your dog feels about you approaching their bowl (and their food) can have a direct impact on how they behave when they come across food outside. If your dog feels threatened when you approach their food, they will be much more likely to gobble it down quickly so you can't take it away and they will feel this way when they find something exciting outside too!

This game aims to help your dog form a positive association with you approaching their bowl. The first rule of this game is that their bowl is never taken away without any prior warning or training. It's also essential that you go at your dog's pace and don't rush through the training process. Rushing won't achieve the desired results any faster; it will just leave your dog open to making more mistakes instead of laying solid foundations for learning.

The second rule of this game is we always add something to the bowl instead of taking anything away. This helps your dog to understand that we are no threat to the food they already have in their bowl. Instead, we deliver super treats to them, which is something they can look forward to as we approach the bowl, instead of learning to dread it!

What You Will Need:
- Bowl
- Your dog's regular food
- Super treats

The Aim Of The Game:
- To change your dog's perception of what it means when you approach their bowl.
- To form a positive association between you approaching their bowl and delivering super treats instead of taking their food away.
- To teach your dog that there is no need to gobble down their food when you approach their bowl because you are not trying to take anything away from them.

NOTE:
If your dog shows any signs of being uncomfortable, stressed, anxious or aggressive at any point, you need to stop this game immediately. This may be displayed as behaviors such as; freezing over the bowl, guarding the food, standing very still with their head lowered, having a stiff/tense body, and staring at you as you approach the bowl. If your dog displays any of these behaviours or if they growl, snap, lunge, or try to protect their bowl from you, you should not continue. If this is the case, you need to contact an experienced dog trainer who uses force-free, positive training methods to help you.

Step 1

Put a small amount of your dog's usual kibble or normal food into their bowl and place it on the floor. Allow your dog to eat from their bowl without any interruptions from you.

Step 2

Once your dog is comfortable eating from their bowl, approach them and give them an informational cue. This could be something like 'Look what I have' or 'What have I got?' When your dog looks up, throw a super treat into their bowl, then step back, leaving them to eat in peace again.

Repeat this step until your dog is comfortably looking up and stepping away from their bowl when you give them your informational cue in anticipation of receiving a super treat.

Step 3

Next, repeat the previous step again. But this time, instead of throwing the super treat into the bowl, crouch down to touch the bowl briefly with one hand, while adding the super treat with your other hand. Step away from the bowl and allow your dog to eat.

Repeat this step until your dog is happy for you to touch their bowl without any signs of uncertainty or stress.

Step 4

Finally, repeat the previous step, but this time, pick up the bowl from the ground, add your super treat, then return the bowl to your dog. Step away and let them eat.

Repeat this step until your dog confidently allows you to take their bowl and return it to them.

NOTE:

At every stage of this game, your dog must always have their bowl returned to them. Never take the bowl away completely, or your dog may start to believe you take things away from them instead of adding higher-value things to them. This is exactly what we are trying to overcome, so it's vital you don't break your dog's trust in you over this. This game's main aim is to change how your dog feels about you approaching their bowl. We want them to learn this is a great thing, not something they want to avoid.

Orientation To Owner Training

Orientation to owner training is not as complicated as it may sound at first! We are simply aiming to get your dog to be able to listen to you successfully when they are out on walks, instead of doing their own thing and obsessively scavenging.

This game encourages your dog to check in with you regularly during their walks. This helps the thinking part of their brain stay engaged with you while they are out and about, instead of their whole brain becoming engrossed in their environment. This allows you to give them cues successfully and helps keep you one step ahead of their scavenging.

How frequently your dog checks in with you gives a clear picture of how they're feeling and, in turn, how they are likely to behave as a result. So, if your dog checks in with you very infrequently or not at all, this suggests they are completely distracted by what is happening around them and will be extremely unlikely to listen to cues successfully. If this is the case, it's best to get your dog back onto their leash or pick up their long line to gain some more control.

If they check in constantly, going no more than a few seconds without looking at you, this isn't ideal either. This means they are not interacting with their environment whatsoever, which is unhealthy for them long term. This stops your dog from behaving as a dog naturally should. They won't sniff, explore, relieve themselves or interact with other people or animals because they are so wrapped up with checking in with you. This is likely to make them feel tense, frustrated, and on edge, which is exactly what you want to avoid when out for a walk!

The ideal scenario is a good balance of both. So, your dog checks in frequently, proving they are engaged with you, but they're still able to do their own thing too. This is exactly what we are trying to encourage and reinforce.

What You Will Need:
- Super treats
- Clicker or marker cue
- Long and/or short leash (for areas where there are higher distractions)

The Aim Of The Game:
- To introduce your dog to checking in and what this means for them.
- To encourage your dog to check in with you regularly on walks.

For orientation training, we have three games that will work simultaneously with each other. All the games should be introduced to your dog in areas with little to no distractions to cement exactly what you are trying to teach them. Once you are confident they have got the hang of it, you can gradually increase the distractions to generalize this behavior.

Simone Mueller

Option 1 – Teaching A Check In

Step 1

Take 10 super treats in the palm of your hand.

Step 2

Place one treat in the other hand and drop it on the floor. Allow your dog to eat it. After this, they will immediately look up at you to see if any more treats are coming their way. Click or say your marker cue at the moment your dog looks up at you.

Step 3

Repeat the previous step, but drop the treat to your opposite side. Alternate right and left until all 10 super treats are used up.

Step 4

Show your dog your empty hands and let them know the game is over, so they don't get frustrated.

Option 2 – Look At Me

Step 1

Choose a cue like 'look' or 'watch' for this game.

Step 2

Say your chosen cue, then your dog's name, mark their eye contact and reward them. So, it would go; 'Look, Meg,' (Meg looks at you), mark this moment and reward.

Step 3

Repeat the previous step until your dog has a solid understanding of what they are being asked to do. Once you are sure they know what you mean, you can leave out their name. So, it would be something like this; Look, (Meg looks at you), mark this moment and reward. This will help pair up your chosen cue with your dog choosing to make eye contact with you.

Step 4

Repeat the previous step until your dog understands it well. Once you are confident, you can gradually increase the number of environmental distractions.

Option 3 - Encouraging Un-Cued Check-Ins

Once your dog is used to the concept of checking in with you, you may find that they naturally offer this behavior much more readily when you are out walking. This game encourages these checks in that your dog has decided to offer themselves, making them more likely to do it again in the future.

Step 1

Walk your dog in an area of low distraction to start with. You can then gradually increase the distraction level once your dog is more confident at this game.

Step 2

Don't give your dog any cues related to checking in. Then, when your dog voluntarily checks in with you, click or use your marker cue to pinpoint this, then throw them a super treat.

NOTE:

They don't have to return all the way back to you as they would with a recall. You are more interested in getting them used to the idea of seeing where you are instead of disappearing entirely into their own little world.

You should practice all three of these games frequently to reinforce to your dog that choosing to make eye contact with you is desirable. These games form the basis of teaching your dog to check in with you when out on a walk.

If you have a dog that constantly checks in with you, to the detriment of them doing anything else on the walk, it's still possible to discourage this behavior without eliminating it entirely. So, instead of rewarding every single check in your dog offers you with a treat, only reward them every 4th or 5th time they offer it.

On the other attempts, you should still acknowledge their check-in attempt, but only with verbal praise instead of a super treat. Saying 'good boy/girl' or 'good job' or even simply nodding or smiling at them, encourages your dog that they are doing the right thing, without them going over the top and doing it constantly!

The Take It Game – Teaching A Release Cue

Teaching a release cue essentially means giving your dog a signal that it is okay for them to eat food they have found on the ground. This helps to provide us with a chance to assess the food they have come across, instead of them rushing to it and gobbling it up before we get there! This way, we can choose whether they can eat it.

Many people believe it's best never to allow your dog to eat anything from the floor, especially if they are well known for scavenging when out and about. However, scavenging is an entirely natural behavior for our dogs. By eliminating it from their day-to-day life altogether, it will only make them crave it even more! Providing them with a suitable outlet for scavenging, which still meets their needs in a safe, controlled way, will be a more successful option than attempting to stop it entirely.

Wild and stray dogs structure their entire day around scavenging. It's a huge part of their daily life, and this is something that our domesticated dogs still deeply desire. If we stop them from scavenging completely, it will only make any discarded food they come across of even higher value to them. They will find it impossible to resist anything they see and will be more likely to grab and devour it, stopping you from taking it away from them. However, teaching them a release cue to signal it is okay for them to eat something can help manage this and give you more control in the process.

What You Will Need:
- Super treats
- Your hand!

Aim Of The Game:
- To teach your dog a release cue that signals they are allowed to eat food from the floor.
- To teach your dog to wait to be given a release cue before taking food they have found.

This game is split into different stages of difficulty. Start with stage one and only progress further when you are sure your dog understands your release cue.

STAGE 1

Step 1

Take a single super treat in the palm of your hand. Then, close your hand into a fist shape.

Step 2

Hold your closed hand in front of your dog and say the cue, 'Take it.'

Step 3

Open your hand to reveal the treat, and allow your dog to eat it.

Once your dog has got the hang of this, and is reliably waiting for your release cue before taking the food, move on to the next stage of this game.

STAGE 2

Step 1

Take a single super treat in the palm of your hand, but this time, leave your hand open flat.

Step 2

Hold your open hand in front of your dog and say the cue, 'Take it.' If your dog tries to take the treat before you give them the release cue, quickly close your hand again to prevent this.

Step 3

Once your dog waits for you to give them the release cue, allow them to eat the treat from your open hand.

Once you are confident your dog understands the meaning of 'take it,' you can increase the difficulty level further.

STAGE 3

Step 1

Take a single super treat and place it on the ground, close to you, allowing your dog to see it.

Step 2

Get your dog to wait a few seconds (don't cue a wait, just quietly let them wait without a cue) before saying, 'Take it.' (The whole aim is getting your dog to wait until you give them the release cue, instead of seeing the food and grabbing it instantly!) Cover the treat with your hand if they try to take it before you give them the release cue.

Step 3

Once your dog waits for you to give them the release cue, allow them to eat the super treat from the ground.

NOTE:

The only exception to this advice would be for owners who are extremely reluctant to let their dog eat from the ground. This may be because they have already had a traumatic experience with their current or previous dog, where they have eaten something poisonous or dangerous, resulting in their dog becoming seriously ill or even dying. If you fall into this category, you can still teach your dog a release cue but pick the food up from the ground and feed it to your dog from your hand instead of the ground. However, whenever possible, it's best to mimic natural scavenging behaviors as closely as possible, which would mean allowing your dog to eat from the floor in a safely managed way.

It's also good practice to only release your dog to the super treat as a bonus intermittently. This reduces the chance of them anticipating this next step and rushing to eat the super treat before you give them the release cue.

Plus, in real-life scenarios, it may not be suitable to release your dog to the super treat for their own safety, so it's important your dog doesn't learn to rush ahead and eat the found food too!

The Core Games of Force-free Food Avoidance Training

A common concern for many owners is what they should do when their dog comes across food on their walk. How should they react? What should you ask your dog to do? Well, this chapter aims to introduce you to three games to teach your dog, which can help you better manage their scavenging when you are out and about. We will look at teaching your dog to stop in front of food, to forget food they have already found, and also to indicate to you that they have found food.

The first of these games is designed to give you more time when your dog discovers discarded food, instead of them rushing ahead and eating it anyway! The other two games are add-ons to the initial game. One is for the scenario where both you and your dog have seen the food. This one allows you to tell them to 'forget it' and move on. The other is for when your dog spots the food before you. This game teaches your dog how to indicate this to you so you can let them know what to do next. The graphic below shows the chain of events and what this means for your dog:

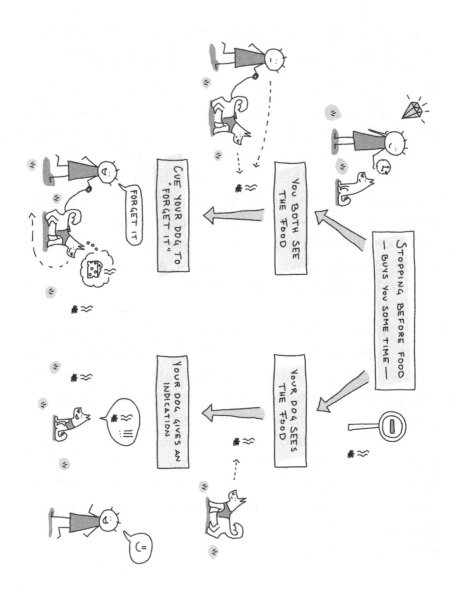

However, it's important to remember that as with all the games recommended in this book, they should remain fun for you and your dog! Keeping training fun and rewarding for both of you is the key to success. As soon as training becomes boring or predictable, your dog will lose interest and switch off, making them much less likely to learn anything.

Ideally, keep your training sessions short and sweet. They should last just 1-3 minutes each time, and you should aim to practice them a couple of times per day. It's surprising how many training opportunities you may miss during a day, and it's easy to make excuses not to do them, but it is certainly more straightforward than you might initially think.

Try to get a training routine going because this will help your dog's success rate and also help them to generalize their learning in different situations. So, don't always practice the same game in the same location. Mix things up and try it in other parts of the house, garden, and at various points on your walks. This helps keep things interesting and encourages your dog to put this training into practice successfully, no matter where they are or what is happening around them.

Humans are creatures of habit, and we tend to stick to what we know. But this can be super boring and frustrating for our dogs, who will quickly lose motivation and interest if we just keep doing the same thing every day. So, mix up your treats and rewards, and don't practice the same game continually in a row. If your dog shows any signs of being frustrated or bored, give training a break or try something else you know they are already good at to build their confidence again.

While training is undoubtedly important if you want to help your dog to control their scavenging, what we don't want is for either yourself or your dog to feel stressed. Try not to approach training like it is a chore because this will make you much less likely to succeed. If you have had a bad day at work and already feel at the end of your tether, it's best to give training a miss for that day until you are in a better mindset. Equally, if your dog has had a stressful day, they too, may not be in the right frame of mind to learn, either. Remember, you always want to set them up for success, not failure! Yes, we want successful training, but we don't want boredom, frustration, or stress because that is not good for either of you!

Stopping Before Food

The aim of this game is to teach your dog to slow down when they find food on the floor and look to you for direction instead of rushing in and eating the food instantly. This gives you time to react appropriately and guide your dog on what to do next.

This is one of the most crucial games of this whole training protocol. So much so, several owners report that they see a considerable improvement in their dog's scavenging behavior by practicing this game. Therefore, if you really commit yourself and put extra effort into practicing this game, you may well see the positive changes you're hoping for. This game is particularly effective for dogs who naturally enjoy cooperating with their owners. Working breeds who tend to be genetically predisposed towards taking guidance from their owners usually breeze through this game with ease! Even if your dog finds this game pretty straight forward, you still need to help them further by generalizing this training in all kinds of different scenarios; this is where the hard work comes in!

What You Will Need:
- So-so treats
- Super treats
- Bowl
- Short Leash
- Clicker or Marker Cue

The Aim Of The Game:
- To teach your dog to slow down when approaching food, they have found.
- To allow you time to react appropriately when your dog finds food.
- To stop your dog from rushing to the food they have found and eating it.

Stopping Before Food Game

This game is split into 4 stages of increasing difficulty. Start at stage 1 and only progress to the following stages when you are confident your dog successfully understands their training.

STAGE 1

Step 1

Put a bowl of so-so treats on the ground and keep your dog on a short, loose leash. Create a distance between your dog and the bowl so they can't reach the treats. You may need to leave a considerable distance to start with to make it easier for your dog to succeed.

Step 2

When your dog looks at the bowl of treats, click or use your marker cue. At this stage, don't move towards the bowl. The aim is for your dog to see the treats, without rushing towards them.

Step 3

Reward your dog with super treats AWAY from the bowl.

Step 4

Repeat this process.

NOTE:

Your leash is only there to prevent your dog from eating the so-so treats as a last resort. You should not consistently let your dog reach the end of their leash. Ideally, it should remain loose at all times. Otherwise, you could accidentally create an association with reaching the end of the leash and getting a reward. You actually want to reward the moment your dog chooses to only look at the food and not eat it. Your clicker or marker cue should act as a positive interrupter so your dog will automatically approach you for a reward when they hear it, thereby choosing to step away from the bowl of treats. The long-term goal of this game is to get your dog to be able to practice it off-leash successfully, so it's best to start this as you mean to go on.

STAGE 2

Step 1

Put a bowl of so-so treats on the ground and keep your dog on a short, loose leash.

Step 2

Allow your dog to look at the bowl, then wait for them to disengage voluntarily. Mark this moment with a click or marker cue.

Step 3

Reward your dog with super treats AWAY from the bowl.

Step 4

Cue 'Take it,' then let your dog eat the so-so treats from the bowl.

Isla is looking at the so-so treats on the ground.

I click/mark her for looking at the food.

I throw a super treat AWAY from the food on the ground.

STAGE 3

Step 1

Put a bowl of so-so treats on the ground and keep your dog on a short, loose leash.

Step 2

Allow your dog to look at the bowl, then wait for them to disengage voluntarily. Mark this moment with a click or marker cue.

Step 3

Reward your dog with super treats AWAY from the bowl.

Step 4

Take a step closer to the bowl and repeat the process. Each time, you take one step closer to the bowl until you are directly in front of it.

NOTE:

If your dog struggles to resist the food, increase the distance between them and the bowl until they can disengage successfully. Remember, your leash should be loose and not the only thing stopping them from eating the food. This is not teaching your dog anything other than the fact their leash prevents them from accessing food they want to eat! Your dog should be voluntarily stopping themselves from eating the food, not relying on their leash, as this won't always be there.

STAGE 4

This stage helps your dog generalize this training in many different situations. This enables them to be successful no matter what is happening in the environment around them. This is perhaps the most challenging part of the training process but the most important. Practice makes perfect, so keep going! Remember, only change one thing at a time, so you don't expect too much of your dog at once.

Here are some suggestions for you to introduce:

- Change the type of food in the bowl - gradually increase the value to make it even more tempting for your dog. Remember that your super treats should always be of higher value than the food in the bowl.
- Train in different locations - Living room, garden, quiet road, road with heavy traffic, woodland, meadow, etc.
- Put the food onto a paper plate or directly onto the ground instead of in a bowl.
- Partially disguise the food with dirt or grass.
- Train at different times of the day - morning, evening, dusk, etc.
- Train in different weathers - rain, wind, sun, snow, etc.
- Simply drop food and use this to practice training.

What Can Go Wrong?

Although this game is relatively straightforward, there are some things that can potentially go wrong. If you are experiencing any problems, take a look at the troubleshooting guide below:

DON'T EAT THAT

Problem:

You are far away from the bowl and still stationary in step 1. Your dog starts to run towards the food as soon as they see it, instead of just looking at it. So, you can't mark the moment they look towards the food.

Solution:

First move: Increase your distance! Most owners underestimate the space that their dog needs to have between them and a trigger. This can apply to reactivity towards other dogs, predation with prey, or in this case, scavenging food on the ground. Often the problem is you are simply too close to the food for them to think properly. So, increase your distance hugely, to begin with! This is the key to success in this game!

Second move: Mark your dog anyway! This might sound bizarre as you are seemingly reinforcing your dog for running towards the food. However, your marker will eventually stop your dog after some repetitions, acting as a positive interrupter. You create a new anticipation as your dog starts running while waiting for the click to interrupt them. You will soon see that your dog will maybe only begin running and then turn around, waiting for your marker. This is the first step.

So, ensure you are far enough away that your dog can't reach the food, and have a helper put the food down. As soon as your dog starts running towards the food, click or give your marker and feed in the OTHER direction, away from the food. Repeat. You should see the hesitation in your dog after a maximum of 10 repetitions.

If you see no improvement, recheck your distance! You might still be too close.

Problem:

Your dog relies on getting to the end of the leash, instead of choosing to stop in front of the food voluntarily.

Solution:

You need to take care to mark the exact moment your dog chooses to voluntarily look away from the food, when their leash is slack. If they are consistently getting to the end of their leash and this is the only thing preventing them from accessing the food, you may need to increase the distance between them and the bowl to make it easier for them.

Problem:

Your dog lunges forward to grab the food as soon as they see it.

Solution:

You need to increase the distance between the bowl and your dog until they can successfully choose to look away from the food. Remember, you should always try to set your dog up for success, not failure! Continually letting your dog fail to do this game correctly won't help them to learn anything; it will just create frustration for them and put them off learning. If your dog is over their threshold, they are not in the right frame of mind to learn new skills.

Problem:

Your dog is only successful at this game in specific situations.

Solution:

You need to work harder on helping your dog generalize this training in different scenarios. Consider the areas you are training in, the food you are using, the rewards you are giving, the time of day, the location, the weather, and any other variables you can think of. If you only ever practice this game in the same location, in similar circumstances, they may not find it possible to do this outside of these parameters.

Problem:

Your dog is making good progress with the game, but then they start to regress.

Solution:

You may be changing too many variables at once. Remember only to change one thing at a time, so you are not expecting too much from your dog in one go. If your dog is struggling, they may be feeling overwhelmed or simply having a bad day. So, it's best to give them a break from training and come back to it another time.

Problem:

Your dog is successful in the game scenario but struggles to succeed when they're out in the 'real world.'

Solution:

Continue your generalization work to ensure your dog understands how to apply their learning in real-life situations. As you know, discarded food on the ground will rarely be found in a dog bowl! So, the aim is to work with a wide selection of foods, presented in different ways until your dog gets the hang of what you are asking them to do.

Forget It – Easy Level

The 'Forget It' game is the next stage of the 'Stopping Before Food' game. This game aims to teach your dog to choose to walk away from food they have found on the ground. This is useful in the scenario when both yourself and your dog have seen the food because it enables you to stop your dog from ignoring you completely and gobbling the food down anyway! It works as a positive interrupter, whereby you use it to stop your dog from eating the found food in exchange for them receiving a higher-value super treat as a reward. It could also be classed as a recall cue, because your dog sees the food, you give them the 'forget it' cue, and they return to you in anticipation of a super treat coming their way! This game creates a much more successful outcome than a standard recall, as it relates specifically to food instead of just being a general recall.

What You Will Need:
- So-so treats
- Super treats
- Short leash
- Clicker or marker cue

The Aim Of The Game:
- To teach your dog to turn away from food they have found on the floor and look to you instead.
- To stop your dog from grabbing the food they have found on the floor and eating it.

Forget It Game – Easy Level

To introduce your dog to the 'forget it' game, you should start at stage 1 of this easier level and progress to stage 2 once they are completing stage 1 successfully. You can then begin to generalize this game once they have got the hang of it. Remember, the aim is to get your dog to disengage from the food they have found on the ground and focus their attention back on you.

STAGE 1

Step 1

Take a so-so treat in one hand and a super treat in the other. Keep the super treat behind your back and leave the so-so treat out in front of you, keeping both hands closed into a fist.

Step 2

Let your dog sniff and lick the hand containing the so-so treat but don't open it!

Step 3

Say 'forget it' in a cheerful voice. This keeps your dog's mind ready for learning instead of approaching them with confrontation, which can scare them.

Step 4

Wait for any sign of your dog disengaging from the so-so treat and as soon as you see it, mark with the clicker or your marker cue and praise them.

NOTE:

In the beginning, this can be any slightest sign of disengagement, such as:

- Your dog is shifting their body backward slightly.
- Your dog is moving their head slightly away from your hand.
- A brief hesitation while your dog thinks about what to do next.

Take any sign of disengagement you see instead of waiting for the more apparent signs to avoid your dog getting frustrated.

Step 5

Bring the super treat hand from behind your back and directly in front of your dog's nose. Encourage them to follow it until they take several steps to the other side of you before they are allowed to eat the super treat. A good rule is that they should walk the length of themselves as this creates distance between the so-so treat, they 'found' and the place where they receive the super treat. This is the main aim here because, in the long run, you want your dog to choose to leave found food alone in return for receiving a super treat from you.

Step 6

While your dog is still eating their super treat, give them your 'take it' cue to let them know they are okay to take the so-so treat as a bonus reward.

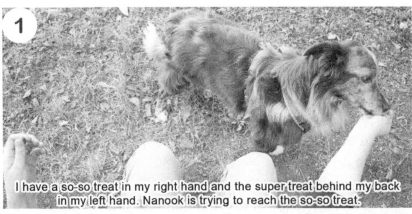

I have a so-so treat in my right hand and the super treat behind my back in my left hand. Nanook is trying to reach the so-so treat.

I say "Forget it!" in a friendly voice and wait for him to show any sign of disengagement.

I click/mark and use the super treat in my left hand to lure him away from the so-so treat in my right hand.

4

I lead him into the opposite direction for at least the length of his body (full disengagement).

5

Only then, I open my hand and feed him the super treat.

6

I immediately give my release cue so that he can have the so-so treat in my right hand as well.

STAGE 2

This stage builds upon stage 1, so the steps are relatively similar:

Step 1

Take a so-so treat in one hand and a super treat in the other. Keep the super treat behind your back and leave the so-so treat out in front of you, keeping both hands closed into a fist.

Step 2

Let your dog sniff and lick the hand containing the so-so treat but don't open it!

Step 3

Say 'forget it' in a cheerful voice. This keeps your dog's mind ready for learning instead of approaching them with confrontation, which can scare them.

Step 4

This time, wait for your dog to disengage from the so-so treat by looking at you.

NOTE:

This is where the game differs from stage 1. So, instead of marking and praising your dog for showing any signs of disengagement, you only do so when they actively choose to look at you.

Some dogs may do this naturally during stage 1, which is excellent! However, other dogs may need you to break it down further to help them succeed. Try marking your dog for looking at your body first, before progressing to them looking at your face, and eventually making eye contact with you.

Step 5

Bring the super treat hand from behind your back and directly in front of your dog's nose. Encourage them to follow it until they take several steps to the other side of you before they are allowed to eat the super treat.

Step 6

While your dog is still eating their super treat, give them your 'take it' cue to let them know they are okay to take the so-so treat as a bonus reward.

STAGE 3

This stage helps you to generalize this game for your dog. This sets them up for success when you need to put it into practice in the outside world. Adding variety to the food you use increases your dog's ability to apply this in real-life situations. Here is what you need to do:

Step 1

Take 5 treats ranging from so-so to super. An example could be:

5. Kibble
4. Bread
3. Cheese
2. Liver
1. Tripe

Step 2

Use number 5 as your so-so treat and number 4 as your super treat.

NOTE:

Start right at the beginning as we did at stage 1, marking any attempt at disengagement no matter how small or subtle it is.

Step 3

Next, use number 4 as your so-so treat and number 3 as your super treat.

Then use number 3 as your so-so treat and number 2 as your super treat.

Then use number 2 as your so-so treat and number 1 as your super treat.

Step 4

Once you are at this stage, you can use a small portion of number 1 as your so-so treat and a larger portion of number 1 as your super treat.

NOTE:

This mimics a real-life scenario, as the food you find on the floor is unpredictable. This means that the super treat you have available may actually be unintentionally of the same value to your dog as the food they find on the floor.

What Can Go Wrong?

If you are having any problems teaching your dog this game, here are some ideas that can help you figure them out:

Problem:

Your dog won't disengage from the hand with the so-so treat inside, not even for a split second. They constantly try to lick, scratch, and nibble their way in to access it, making your hand sore and getting them frustrated in the process.

Solution:

Option 1: You could try wearing gardening gloves to stop your dog from injuring your hand. This means you can still move your hand freely and feel what you are doing, while protecting your hand from teeth and claws!

Then, you mark any tiny, subtle attempt at disengagement. This could be when your dog pulls their ears back, looks towards the floor, looks slightly to one side of your hand, shifts their body backward slightly, or if they hesitate briefly.

Anything which suggests they are choosing not to get the so-so treat from your closed hand.

Option 2: Another way to overcome this is to consider the value of your chosen so-so treat. It could be that your dog values it more than you realized, which makes their life much harder at this early stage. Try something like celery, apple, or something else plain and low-value.

Option 3: Try lifting your hand slightly out of your dog's reach. This does two things; firstly, it relieves some of the frustration involved for dogs who struggle with the concept of 'this is being handed to me, why can't I get to it?!' Secondly, it tends to inevitably create a moment where the dog shifts their weight backwards slightly, for their own comfort, which allows you to mark and reward this movement away from the hand.

If frustration continues to build and your dog is still unsuccessful, take a break to do another activity, then return to this game. Allowing your dog's frustration levels to rise continually will not set them up for success!

Problem:

Your dog doesn't follow your hand containing the super treat, so you cannot create distance from the so-so treat hand.

Solution:

Use encouraging noises to make your super treat hand even more appealing to your dog. Silly, high-pitched, fun-sounding sounds like kissing noises or 'pup, pup, pup' can work well for this, as this is likely to get your dog's interest.

It's also a good idea to make your super treat, even more super! It may be as simple as your dog not finding your chosen super treat enticing enough, so you might need to increase its value. Choose a treat that is even smellier and more attractive to your dog, like smoked cheese, tuna, liver paste, etc., that they will find impossible to resist. Refer back to the original list you made of treats your dog loves to get some inspiration.

When you have this super treat in your hand, it should act like a magnet for your dog's nose, so as soon as it's in front of their snout, they should be lured by it wherever you go!

Problem:

Your dog eats the super treat, and then immediately grabs the so-so treat before you give them the release cue.

Solution:

Keep the hand containing the so-so treat closed! Then your dog simply can't access it anyway! However, in order to prevent this from becoming an issue in the future, follow these steps:
1. Say the release cue 'take it.'
2. Then give the hand gesture to show your dog where the food is they can take. (dogs tend to naturally prioritize hand gestures as they often respond better to our body language than they do to verbal cues)
3. Open the hand with the so-so treat in and let your dog eat it.

NOTE:

Only give your release cue of 'take it' as your dog finishes the last part of their super treat. Never give the release cue when your dog is already making their way towards the so-so treat, as this teaches them to pre-empt what you are about to say to them, leaving your release cue useless!

DON'T EAT THAT

Problem:

Your dog only momentarily disengages with the so-so treat, just long enough to gulp the super treat, before rushing back to eat the so-so treat too.

Solution:

You should only give your dog the super treat when they have made the conscious decision to move a fair distance away from the so-so treat. Don't release them to the so-so treat until their whole body has moved away from your so-so treat hand. Getting them to move their entire body, not just their head, helps them fully disengage properly, including their mind.

Some dogs may forget about the so-so treat because they're so interested in getting his super treat instead. This is ideal as it proves they have become totally disinterested in the so-so treat that they were once so keen to access!

Forget It - Intermediate Level

Once your dog fully understands the basic concept of the 'forget it' game and can execute it successfully, it is time to move on to the intermediate level of training. This level of the 'forget it' game is similar in principle to the easy level but is just slightly more challenging for your dog. This stage helps your dog begin to apply their learning to scenarios that are closer to reality, instead of just solely in a training setup.

What You Will Need:
- So-so treats
- Super treats
- Short leash
- Clicker or marker cue
- Fast reactions!

The Aim Of The Game:
- To teach your dog to actively choose to leave food they have found on the floor.
- To encourage your dog to return to you for a high-value reward instead of choosing to eat the food they have found.

Forget It Game - Intermediate Level

Step 1

Sit on the floor or a chair, hold a super treat in one hand and place it behind your back.

Step 2

Place a so-so treat on the ground near you, but far enough away so your dog can't access it. The so-so treat should be uncovered on the floor, as it would be in a real-life scenario.

NOTE:

It would be helpful if your dog were still on a leash at this point; however, this shouldn't be the only thing preventing them from accessing the treat. The leash is only a backup in case your dog tries to grab the treat, and you are not quick enough to stop them! Always attach your leash to a harness and not a collar. Then, if your dog lunges forward suddenly, they are at a much lower risk of damaging their delicate neck.

Step 3

Click or mark if your dog looks at the so-so treat on the floor but doesn't attempt to take it. Say the cue 'forget it' to create an association with seeing the food on the ground and choosing not to take it.

NOTE:

If your dog tries to immediately pounce on the so-so treat, quickly cover it with your hand to prevent them from accessing it. If they still struggle to succeed, create more distance between them and the so-so treat on the ground to make the game a little easier for them.

Step 4

Reward your dog with the super treat from behind your back, a good few steps away from the so-so treat on the ground.

NOTE:

As a general rule, your dog should move away from the treat on the ground at least the length of their body before eating the super treat from your hand. This encourages them to actively move away from enticing things on the ground, which will eventually become a habit and a part of the cue.

Make sure your dog knows what they have just chosen to do is a fantastic decision! So really reward and praise them well for choosing to forget the food on the floor. This will make it much more likely for them to do this again in the future!

Step 5

Give your dog the release cue of 'take it' while they are still eating the super treat, to signal that they can then eat the so-so treat as a bonus reward.

Repeat this process until your dog is successful every time.

1. The so-so treat is on the ground and the super treat behind my back in my left hand. Nanook is looking at the so-so treat on the ground.

2. I mark for looking at the treat but not trying to get it and say "Forget it!" in a friendly voice.

3. I bring the super treat from behind my back and lure him away from the so-so treat on the ground.

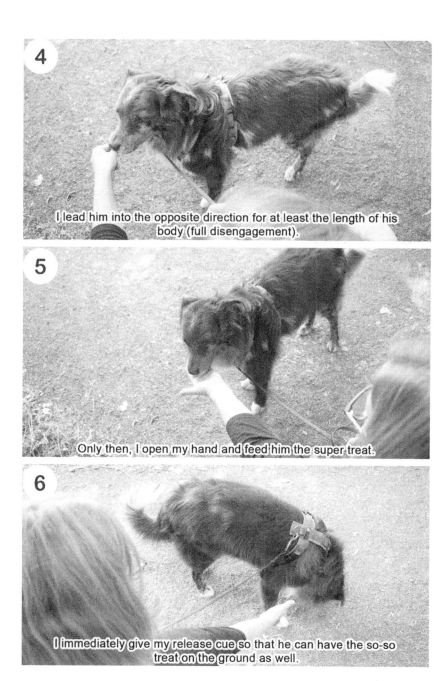

4

I lead him into the opposite direction for at least the length of his body (full disengagement).

5

Only then, I open my hand and feed him the super treat.

6

I immediately give my release cue so that he can have the so-so treat on the ground as well.

109

Step 6

Now it's time to stand up and do the game again from a standing position. Start from a reasonable distance away from the so-so treat on the ground.

NOTE:

It's helpful to have a helper here who puts the so-so treats down for you. If you don't have a helper, you may find it helpful to tie your dog to a tree or fence and put the treat down yourself. Now repeat steps 1 to 5 from a standing position.

Step 7

Then, once your dog is successfully completing the game with you in a standing position, you can gradually increase the difficulty by moving slowly closer towards the so-so treat each time. Eventually, you should be able to stand directly in front of the so-so treat, with a loose leash, cue 'forget it,' and your dog should be able to respond appropriately.

What Can Go Wrong?

If your dog seems to be struggling with this game, here are some ideas that may help you out:

Problem:

Your dog immediately tries to pounce on the so-so treat on the ground and cannot disengage from it whatsoever.

Solution:

Create more distance between your dog and the so-so treat on the floor. If your dog is significantly over their threshold, it will be almost impossible for them to think about what they are doing. Their whole brain will be taken over by the desire to eat the food! Increasing the distance between them and the so-so treat can help them think more clearly, which sets them up for success.

You should also consider the value of your so-so treat and, if possible, swap it for something of even lower value to start with.

Problem:

Your dog lunges to the end of their leash, which is the only thing preventing them from accessing the so-so treat on the ground.

Solution:

Consider the length of your leash. It may be best to start with a shorter leash, to begin with, before giving your dog the responsibility of a longer leash. There should be enough distance between your dog and the so-

so treat that even if they reach the end of their leash, they still can't access the treat itself.

So, if they reach the end of their leash, don't move! Instead, remain exactly where you are and wait for your dog to show some disengagement signals voluntarily. As soon as they do, click and reward with the super treat but don't go on to release them to the so-so treat as a bonus.

Forget It – Expert Level

The expert level of the 'forget it' game builds upon what your dog has already learned in the intermediate level of training. So, once you are sure they are ready, you can progress to this stage to really push their training further. This will help prepare your dog for what they should do in a real-life setting.

What You Will Need:
- So-so treats
- Super treats
- Clicker or marker cue
- Plastic tub/can/bird feeder/humane mouse traps/ anything else that you can use to put food in securely

NOTE: Whatever you choose should be secure but not totally air-tight. This allows your dog to smell the so-so treat, without having direct access to it to begin with.

The Aim Of The Game:
- To build upon the learning your dog has already done in the intermediate level of training.
- To teach your dog to successfully leave food they have found on the floor, even when they are off the leash.

Forget It Game – Expert Level

The expert level follows the same basics as the intermediate level of training. This time though, your dog should be off leash completely. You will then progress through several stages, each increasing in difficulty, until you mimic different real-life scenarios.

STAGE 1

Step 1

Sit on the floor and hold a super treat in one hand and place it behind your back.

Step 2

Place a so-so treat in a lidded tub on the ground near to you.

Step 3

Click or mark if your dog looks at the so-so treat on the floor, but doesn't attempt to take it. Say the cue 'forget it' to create an association with seeing the food on the ground and choosing not to take it.

NOTE:

Even if your dog tries to access the so-so treat, they shouldn't be able to do so, as it should be securely fastened into the plastic tub or other vessels you are using.

Step 4

Reward your dog with the super treat from behind your back, a good few steps away from the so-so treat on the ground.

NOTE:

Although we mentioned this in the intermediate level, it's important to remember that as a general rule, your dog should move away from the treat on the ground at least the length of their body before getting to eat the super treat from your hand. This encourages them to actively move away from enticing things on the ground, and this will eventually become a habit and a part of the cue.

Make sure your dog knows what they have just chosen to do is a fantastic decision! So really reward and praise them well for choosing to forget the food on the floor. This will make it much more likely for them to do this again in the future!

Step 5

Give your dog the release cue of 'take it' while they are still eating the super treat, to signal that they can then eat the so-so treat as a bonus reward.

Repeat this process until your dog is successful every time.

NOTE:

You should only give your dog the release cue to take the so-so treat if they have responded to your 'forget it' cue the first time.

DON'T EAT THAT

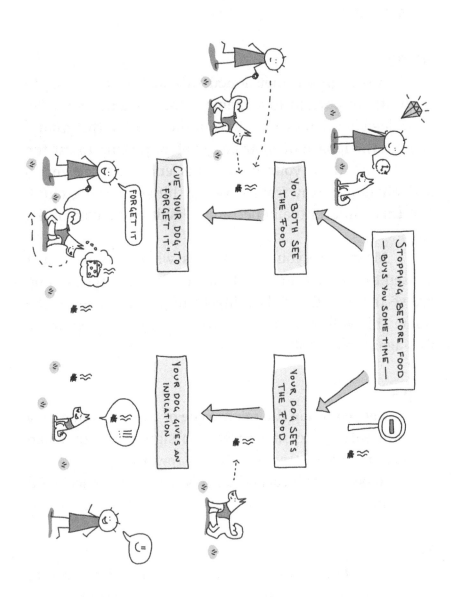

STAGE 2

Repeat steps 1 to 5 but this time, don't securely fasten the lid to the tub; only place it on the top loosely. This lets more scent out of the tub, which will be more enticing for your dog.

STAGE 3

Repeat steps 1 to 5, but this time, remove the lid and replace it with a thin cloth. Again, this allows more scent to leave the tub, but the visual aspect of the so-so treat is still obscured.

STAGE 4

Repeat steps 1 to 5 but this time, remove the cloth, so the so-so treat is loose inside the tub but is now uncovered.

STAGE 5

Repeat steps 1 to 5 but this time, remove the so-so treat from the container altogether, just leaving it loose on the floor.

STAGE 6

Repeat steps 1 to 5 but each time, change the value of your so-so and super treats. An example could be:

5. Kibble
4. Bread
3. Cheese
2. Liver
1. Tripe

Use number 5 as your so-so treat and number 4 as your super treat.

Next, use number 4 as your so-so treat and number 3 as your super treat.

Then use number 3 as your so-so treat and number 2 as your super treat.

Then use number 2 as your so-so treat and number 1 as your super treat.

Once your dog is successful at this stage, you can use a small portion of number 1 as your so-so treat and a larger portion of number 1 as your super treat.

NOTE:

This mimics a real-life scenario, as the food you find on the floor is unpredictable. This means that the super treat you have available may actually be unintentionally of the same value to your dog as the food they find on the floor

STAGE 7

Now it's time for generalization of this training. You need your imagination for this stage! Create as many different scenarios that replicate real life as you can. Some suggestions for things to think about could be:

- **Location** - Your home, garden, on the street outside your house, on a walk, near a school, on a retail park, in a field, at the dog park, on a quiet street, on a busier street, near a fast-food restaurant, anywhere where you can think of!
- **Time** - Morning, evening, before your dog's meals, after they've been fed, at the start of the walk, at

the end of a walk, as soon as you step out the door, as many different times of day as possible.

- **Weather** - when it's raining, sunny, cold, snowy, windy, as many different weather scenarios as possible.
- **Treats** – Change up the so-so and super treats you use regularly; you never know what you might come across in a real-life situation. You can even use burgers, sandwiches, pizza, kebabs, chips, or anything you are more likely to come across in reality.
- **Presentation** – Think about how your dog may find food on the ground. So, in a paper bag, wrapped in foil, in a pizza box, in a takeaway wrapper, on a paper plate, wrapped in cling film, in a plastic bag and of course, just loose on the floor etc.
- **Placement** - Consider how the food will be placed; try dropping the food near to your dog, letting them find it when they are far in front of you, allowing them to find it when they are near to you, and getting a helper to place the food for you. Also, think about where it is placed, in the grass, on the pavement, in a hedge etc.

What Can Go Wrong?

Problem:

Your dog immediately tries to pounce on the so-so treat, or tries to break into the container and is unable to disengage from it at all.

Solution:

Create more distance between your dog and the so-so treat in the container. If your dog is significantly over their threshold, it will be almost impossible for them to think about what they are doing; their whole brain will be taken over by the desire to eat the food! Increasing the distance between them and the so-so treat can help them think more clearly, which sets them up for success.

You should also consider the value of your so-so treat and, if possible, swap it for something of even lower value to start with.

Problem:

Your dog is successful during the earlier stages but struggles when the visibility and scent of the so-so treat are increased.

Solution:

Simply go back a stage and really cement your dog's learning at this stage before moving onto stages with more incredible difficulty. Letting your dog continually get it wrong will only lead to frustration which will not put them in the right frame of mind for learning.

Forget It - In Real Life

Once you have done the groundwork for your "forget it' training, it's time to transfer it into your day-to-day life. This is the most crucial step to training, as, without this, your dog won't be able to generalize their learning enough to be able to apply it to real-life settings.

So, you should ideally always have a super treat ready whenever you walk your dog. This way, you are always prepared to reward them when they come across something on the floor, and they respond to you when you ask them to 'Forget it.' Don't be afraid to get creative with your super treat options! After all, the temptations your dog will encounter in the outside world will be much greater than in the more controlled training environment.

The main criteria for your super treats are that they should be easy to carry around with you in your treat pouch, easy for you to open to access them quickly, and have a long shelf life so they won't go off too quickly. Avoid fresh foods which will promptly go off and instead choose something that will last a long time when it's unopened, but is still delicious for your dog. This way, you can be sure always to have access to a super treat, no matter when you might need it.

Some super treat suggestions include:

- **Canned Food** - Choose cans with a ring pull top, so you can open them quickly when you need the super treat. Tuna, corned beef, steak chunks, sardines, etc., are all excellent options.
- **Pouches Of Cat Food** - Because cats are more taste sensitive than dogs, their food often contains more artificial flavors to encourage them to eat. So, dogs often find cat food irresistible! Plus, you can quickly open a pouch of cat food when you need a super treat, and they're not too heavy to carry with you.
- **Squeezy Or Spray Cheese** - These can come in tubes or cans, and you are able to squeeze out just the amount you need for a super treat reward.

If you get caught out without a super treat to hand, you can make up for this by increasing the volume of the so-so treats you give to your dog if you have those with you. Instead of just giving them one or two so-so treats, throw a whole handful of them into the air, so they shower down to the ground all around your dog. Pair this with lots of high-pitched, excitable praise for your dog, so they know they have done a great thing, and you are really pleased with them!

If you don't have any treats with you, you could play a game with your dog that you know they love instead. You could run with them, so they chase you or play a search game with their favorite toy. Whatever you choose to do, make sure it's exciting and rewarding for your dog. They have got to know you are ecstatic they have decided to move away from the food on the ground and come to you instead.

If you find yourself in a situation where your dog finds food on the ground, and you need to use your 'Forget It' cue in real life, you should follow this up with 2 or 3 intentional sessions where your super treats are exceptionally super. This keeps your dog's faith in you, that what you have to offer them is always the best option, no matter what they have found on the floor.

The whole foundation of the 'Forget It' training rests on the basis that your dog trusts you to always have a super treat of higher value than whatever they have found on the ground. It's essential you maintain this level of trust, so your dog knows that this will always be the case, no matter what they come across in the real world.

Show Me What You Found

The 'Show Me What You Found' game is the third core game involved in managing your dog's scavenging. This game teaches your dog what they should do if they come across food on the floor before you are aware of it. By the end of this game, your dog will be providing you with a clear indication that they have found something to eat. This then gives you the opportunity to investigate what they have found and give them something safe instead.

What You Will Need:
- Leash
- Super treats
- So-so treats
- Clicker or marker cue
- Plastic tub/can/bird feeder/humane mouse traps/ anything else that you can use to put food in securely

NOTE: Whatever you choose should be secure but not totally air-tight. This allows your dog to smell the so-so treat, without having direct access to it, to begin with.

The Aim Of The Game:
- To encourage your dog to indicate to you that they have found something interesting on the floor.
- To set your dog up for success in real-life scenarios, where they find food on the floor before you see it.

'Show Me What You Found' Game

First of all, you need to choose an indication behavior that is both easy for your dog to execute and easy for you to recognize quickly too. A good example to use would be 'Sit.' This is because the vast majority of dogs are already familiar with this and understand what it means. It's also likely to have already been well generalized in lots of different situations, which gives your dog a higher chance of being able to show it successfully, no matter what is going on around them.

NOTE:

The only time that Sit would not be a suitable option, is for dogs who already have known issues with their hips or other joints, which can make it more uncomfortable to get into the sitting position. If this is the case, you could teach them to bark as an indication instead, or choose a different behavior which they can execute more readily. For this, it's best to contact a force-free dog trainer in your area who can help you teach your dog this successfully. Using more complex behaviors as indicators is generally more challenging to teach, so you would likely benefit from the help of a knowledgeable, positive trainer here.

STAGE 1

Step 1

To start with, you should repeat the 'Stopping Before Food' game with your dog on a leash. Gradually decrease the distance between your dog and the so-so treat on the ground, until you are around 30cm away from it.

By this point, your dog should have a good understanding of what to do here, so they should know to stop in front of the food and look at it, but not try to access it.

Step 2

At this point, instead of marking your dog for simply looking at the food and not trying to take it (as you would have done in the Stopping Before Food game), you ask them to Sit.

NOTE:

The process is exactly the same as the Stopping Before Food game, only this time, you also ask your dog to Sit.

Step 3

If your dog responds to your Sit cue successfully, immediately mark this, step away from the so-so treat on the floor and reward your dog with a super treat. Then, give your release cue to allow them to eat the so-so treat as a bonus.

Nanook is looking at the so-so treats on the ground.

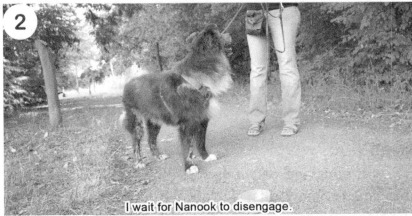

I wait for Nanook to disengage.

I ask Nanook to sit.

I click/mark and lead him with a super treat away from the food on the ground.

I reward him with a super treat and immediately send him back to have the so-so treats on the ground as well.

STAGE 2

Step 1

For the next stage of this training, you should repeat steps 1-3 of Stage 1. But, instead of cueing a Sit in step 2, you wait a few seconds when your dog is in front of the food, to see if they offer to sit voluntarily.

Step 2

If your dog understands that you want them to sit, and does so without a cue, mark this, step away from the so-so treat and reward them with your super treat. You can then use your release cue so they can eat the so-so treat as a bonus.

NOTE:

If your dog does not yet understand that you want them to sit, and they don't do it voluntarily after a few seconds, you can give them the Sit cue. Mark and reward them with a super treat when they are successful here, but don't release them to the so-so treat as a bonus. Then, return to Stage 1 for more repetitions to ensure your dog fully understands what to do.

STAGE 3

This stage helps to prolong your dog's indication behavior for a longer length of time. This helps them prepare for real-life scenarios, where you may not always be able to reward them immediately; they may have to wait a few seconds for you to catch up with them.

Step 1

When your dog is successfully sitting in front of the so-so treat on the floor, without any cues to do so, count to 3 seconds in your head before you mark and reward them with a super treat.

Step 2

Once your dog can successfully wait 3 seconds, repeat the exercise but add another second onto their waiting time, so they are sitting for 4 seconds before you mark and reward them with a super treat.

Continue this process, but only ever add 1 second each time. Even if your dog is doing very well with this exercise, don't be tempted to add more than a second in one go, as this is more likely to set your dog up for failure, instead of success.

STAGE 4

Once your dog successfully understands this exercise and is reliably sitting for several seconds in front of food they find on the floor, you can repeat the exercise with them off the leash.

However, when your dog is off the leash, make sure you have secured the so-so treat on the ground in a container that your dog can't access directly.

- First have the so-so treat in a secure container, with holes in the lid and repeat the exercise.
- Next, have the so-so treat in a secure container without a lid, but with a cloth covering the top and repeat the exercise.

- Then, remove the so-so treat from the container, leaving it directly on the floor and repeat the exercise.

NOTE:

Only move on to the more difficult stages of this game if you are certain your dog fully understands what they need to do. If you try and rush to get through the different stages of difficulty too quickly, then your dog is much less likely to be successful. Putting in the groundwork now with this game, will set you and your dog up for success in real-life settings, so it's important you get it right!

STAGE 5

This is the generalization stage, where you practice the game in as many different situations as you can possibly think of. This helps your dog to understand and realize they should always show their indication behavior no matter what environment they are in, or what they have found on the floor.

NOTE:

Always make sure that the super treat you have to reward your dog is always at least one step higher than the so-so treat you leave on the ground. If this is not possible, use a higher volume of so-so treats as a reward instead.

Here is a reminder of the types of things you need to think about to generalize this game thoroughly:

- **Location** - Your home, garden, on the street outside your house, on a walk, near a school, on a retail park, in a field, at the dog park, on a quiet street, on a busier street, near a fast-food restaurant, anywhere where you can think of!
- **Time** - Morning, evening, before your dog's meals, after they've been fed, at the start of the walk, at the end of a walk, as soon as you step out the door, as many different times of day as possible.
- **Weather** - when it's raining, sunny, cold, snowy, windy, as many different weather scenarios as possible.
- **Treats** - Change up the so-so and super treats you use regularly; you never know what you might come across in a real-life situation. You can even use burgers, sandwiches, pizza, kebabs, chips, or anything you are more likely to come across in reality.
- **Presentation** - Think about how your dog may find food on the ground. So, in a paper bag, wrapped in foil, in a pizza box, in a takeaway wrapper, on a paper plate, wrapped in clingfilm, in a plastic bag, and of course, just loose on the floor etc.
- **Placement** - Consider how the food will be placed; try dropping the food near to your dog, letting them find it when they are far in front of you, allowing them to find it when they are near to you, and getting a helper to place the food for you. Also, think about where it is placed, in the grass, on the pavement, in a hedge etc.

What Can Go Wrong?

There are a few issues you might face along the way, but here are the ways to solve them:

Problem:

You can't release your dog to the food they have found in real life because it may be dangerous or poisonous for them.

Solution:

If you come across food on the floor in reality, you should really celebrate with your dog for them carrying out their indication successfully and choosing to leave the food behind in exchange for a higher value reward from you instead. Make sure you show lots of excitement and happiness so not only does your dog know they have done a great thing, but they may also get so caught up in the celebrations that they could forget about the food they found anyway!

Because you have always rewarded your dog with a super treat away from the food they have found, this naturally creates distance between them and the food on the floor. This can give you the opportunity to put them back on the leash and lead them away from the temptation of the food if they really can't forget about it!

Also, if this happens, it's a good idea to set up an intentional training scenario the following day, where your dog is allowed to be released to the so-so treat on the ground as a bonus reward. This helps recharge your dog's learning and the faith they have in the game, always working out in their favor.

Problem:

Your dog becomes frustrated when you try to prolong their indication behavior and loses interest in playing the game or starts trying to break their sit before you release them.

Solution:

Just because your dog is doing well prolonging their sit when they are in front of the food, doesn't mean you have to keep continually pushing them to do it for longer and longer. In fact, it's better to let them have some 'easy wins' every so often so they are not always faced with something that is getting more and more difficult for them to do each time. For example, if they are successfully holding their sit position for 10 seconds, the next time you try, only ask them to do it for 5 seconds. This way, they are still successful, and you are still cementing their learning, without the continual increase in difficulty. It is best to quit while you are ahead sometimes and only do 3 or 4 of these repetitions really well, before moving on to something else, so your dog doesn't start getting bored or frustrated.

Problem:

You know where the food will be on the floor in a training situation, as you are likely to have put it there yourself! This could mean that you are inadvertently giving your dog subtle clues when they are getting close to the food. You may slow down slightly, hold your breath, or move your hand, quite often without knowing you are doing it at all! Your dog can then become dependent on these subtle accidental clues, instead of coming across the food naturally as they would in real life.

Solution:

If you are working alone, it can be helpful to film yourself working to see exactly what you are doing. Sometimes these clues are so subtle that you might not consciously know you are doing it, but chances are your dog will notice them! You can then watch the video back to see for yourself if you are giving your dog any clues and make an effort to avoid doing so next time.

Or, if you have a helper available, you can get them to lay the food down on the ground so that both you and your dog won't know where it will be located. This would be a 'double blind' exercise where you wouldn't be able to give accidental clues if you don't know where the food is either.

Problem:

Dogs with exceptionally high levels of intelligence may be able to differentiate between a training scenario and a real-life setting. So, they may learn not to show interest in the food they come across in training sessions, as they know it's been placed there by you! But they'll still attempt to access the food they find, out in the real world.

Solution:

Food you have touched will undoubtedly have your scent all over it, which is a massive indicator to your dog that you have been involved in putting it there. Instead, try wearing disposable gloves to handle the food, or use tweezers or tongs to lift it from the container. You could also pour the food directly onto the ground from the container, without actually touching it directly.

If possible, it's a good idea to get a helper to lay food out for your training sessions, that they have bought there themselves, without your physical input. Then, this way, your scent won't be involved at all! This too, will act as a 'double-blind' exercise where both you and your dog won't know where the food is, which would mimic reality much more closely. This way, you would not give your dogs any extra clues to let them know you are aware where the food is either.

Emergency Cue – Open Your Mouth

The overall aim of the training games within this book is to teach your dog not to pick up food they come across on the floor. However, if you are still at the very beginning of your training journey, you will likely find yourself in a scenario where you need to open your dog's mouth to remove something they have picked up. This is a valuable emergency cue to teach your dog, even if they are well on their way with their scavenging management training. After all, even a highly trained dog may have moments where their training is not as reliable as you would like!

Many owners fall into the trap of chasing after their dog, grabbing them, and forcing their mouth open in an attempt to remove something they have found on the floor. However, even if this works once or twice, it's not a good idea to do this long-term. Given the opportunity, your dog will become much faster than you and swallow anything immediately if they think you are about to take it away. Some dogs may also show aggression towards their owner to try and protect the food they have found from being 'stolen' from them.

So, the aim of teaching your dog to open their mouth without instantly swallowing whatever they have found, is to give you the opportunity to consensually remove it from their mouth in return for a higher value reward.

What You Will Need:
- Super treats
- Clicker or marker cue

The Aim Of The Game:
- To teach your dog to feel comfortable with you opening their mouth to remove scavenged food from it safely.
- To create cooperation between you and your dog when they have picked up food from the ground, and you need them to release it.

'Open Your Mouth' – Game

Step 1

Give your dog an information cue such as 'Open Your Mouth.'

Keep your hands in your pocket as you give this cue; wait at least 1 second after giving the cue before removing your hands and moving them towards your dog's muzzle.

There should be a notable gap between giving the information cue and you actually reaching towards your dog's muzzle. Without this pause, it would no longer be an information cue, warning your dog what is about to happen, because it would already be happening!

NOTE:

The information cue gives your dog a chance to prepare themself for you physically opening their mouth. This helps your dog be prepared for what is about to happen, so it is not surprising or alarming for them when you do so. In the same way a Dentist wouldn't immediately start drilling your teeth as soon as you sat in the chair. They would explain the procedure and ensure you were comfortable and consented to it first. Although it is not likely to be a particularly pleasant experience for you, it's short-lived and in your best interests. Forewarning you first allows you to brace yourself for what is about to happen; this is precisely the same principle for your dog.

Step 2

Touch your dog's muzzle with your hand but only do so if they feel comfortable. Don't try and open their mouth straight away; you can build up to this part slowly, so that you don't overwhelm them.

NOTE:

If your dog shows any signs of discomfort or stress, take a step back and progress even slower. It's essential that this training remains fun and comfortable for your dog at all times, or else they may start to feel uneasy about you handling their mouth or approaching their face, which is the exact opposite of what you want to happen!

Step 3

Mark the touch of your dog's muzzle while your hand is still touching them. Reward your dog with a super treat, then remove your hand.

NOTE:

This acts as a double reward! One is the addition of a tasty super treat (reward 1), and the second is the removal of your hand, which will make your dog more comfortable (reward 2)

Step 4

This step is split into several smaller steps, which you can progress through at your dog's own rate. Don't try and rush, though; you want them to feel comfortable throughout each part! So, once your dog is comfortable with your hand touching their muzzle, progress to the following:

- Hand on their muzzle, applying slightly more pressure
- One hand above their muzzle and the second one below, under their jaw
- Pressing lightly around their teeth and mouth
- Moving their lips slightly to expose their gums and teeth
- Gently opening their mouth enough to touch their tongue
- Carefully opening their mouth wider

Once your dog is happy for you to gently open their mouth to create a reasonable opening, place a small super treat directly onto their tongue and let them close their mouth again. This will prove to your dog that great things happen when they allow you to open their mouth briefly!

What Could Go Wrong?

Problem:

In training, you add a tasty treat to your dog's mouth, but in reality, you would be removing something delicious from their mouth. This can make your dog lose faith that something good will happen when you take their found food away from them.

Solution:

Always make sure that you reward your dog with a very high-value treat once you have had to remove something from their mouth. This will hopefully encourage them that they still get something good out of allowing you to remove something from their mouth.

Also, when you have had to use this emergency cue in real life, try and set up some training scenarios the next day to essentially recharge this cue for your dog. This will restore their faith in you that you add delicious things to their mouth, much more often than you take them away.

Emergency Cue - Drop It

Teaching your dog a reliable and instant 'drop it' cue is an extremely useful skill for them to have. This is particularly helpful if your dog is still in the early stages of their training. However, even a more experienced dog may still forget their training occasionally, in which case you need to get them to drop whatever they have in their mouth!

To teach your dog a 'drop it' cue, we will use classical conditioning methods to train them. In this case, your dog will learn to immediately open their mouth, when they hear your 'drop it' cue. This is an example of a behavior learned unconsciously via classical conditioning. This method creates a 'whiplash' response where your dog will respond instantly upon hearing the cue. The only way to train this cue reliably and kindly is via classical conditioning, hence why it is so beneficial here.

However, for this training to be successful, you need to have excellent reactions. For your dog to effectively learn the 'drop it' cue, you need to pair the cue and your response to it in between 1 and 1.5 seconds! This helps to create a sense of urgency for your dog, who will quickly realize they should respond instantly to your cue without having to think about it first.

What You Will Need:
- So-so treats
- Super treats
- Low-value items such as a book, umbrella, bottle, plant pot, shoe, etc.) Anything your dog will show a small amount of interest in, but not want actually to pick up into their mouth
- Low-value dog toys
- High-value dog toys

The Aim Of The Game:
- To teach your dog how to immediately drop whatever is in their mouth when you give them the cue.
- To give you a reliable emergency cue to efficiently and quickly get your dog to drop what they have in their mouth.

'Drop It' - Game

Step 1

Begin in an area where there are no distractions for your dog whatsoever. They should also have nothing in their mouth at this point.

Say 'Drop' and immediately throw treats directly in front of your dog's nose. This should take them by surprise almost, as they should not be expecting you to do this.

NOTE:

Remember, the time between you saying Drop and you throwing the treats, should be 1 - 1.5 seconds only. So, you need to be fast! Make sure your treats are easily accessible, and you don't have to fiddle around with a plastic bag or drawstring pouch to access them quickly.

However, don't put your hand on the treats or in your treat pouch before you say the Drop cue, as this will create anticipation for your dog, who will then realize something is about to happen.

Use your hand to push the treats closer to your dog and help them to make sure they have found them all.

Although this may not sound particularly important, it actually plays a vital role. During the later stages of this training and in real-life scenarios, you will need to remove the item your dog drops from their mouth. For this, you will need your dog to feel comfortable with your hand approaching them to remove it. So, introducing our hand at this early stage, teaches them that your hand is a part of this process. They will also see it positively, as your hand is helping them to access extra tasty treats, instead of trying to take things away from them.

However, if your dog shows any signs of aggression during this stage, stop the training and contact a force-free dog trainer or behaviorist for advice.

Next, you need to generalize this step extremely well before progressing to the next one. Do this while you are sitting down, standing up, close to your dog, further away from them, on your phone, tying your shoelaces, moving around, standing still, while your dog is sitting, while they are lying down, while they are moving around, etc.

Repeat this step in as many different scenarios as possible, all in areas of low distraction, until your dog reliably looks to the floor immediately after giving them the Drop cue.

Step 2

Take an item of low value (a book, bottle, umbrella, shoe, plant pot, etc.) and place it on the floor.

Your dog will likely want to sniff it, so as soon as they start investigating it, give your Drop cue, then throw treats directly under their nose. Don't forget to use your hand to push the treats closer to them.

NOTE:

This adds to the level of distraction, without expecting your dog to physically drop anything from their mouth just yet. We will build up to this later in the following steps.

Now, generalize this step with as many low-value items as you can find in as many different low-distraction environments as you can. Take your time with this to make sure your dog fully understands what it means when you give them the Drop cue, no matter where they are.

Once your dog is reliably turning away from the item and looking to the floor immediately after you give them the Drop cue, you can move on to the next step.

Step 3

Take a lower-value dog toy, something your dog likes, but doesn't go wild for.

Encourage them to pick it up and hold it in their mouth, then give the Drop cue and throw treats under their nose. Then push the treats closer to their mouth to help them find them.

NOTE:

By this point, your dog should automatically open their mouth to drop the toy when you give them the Drop cue. If they don't, go back a step to make sure they really understand what you are asking them to do.

Even when your dog has dropped the toy to the floor, don't actually remove it from them altogether.

You should only completely remove whatever they have dropped in an emergency situation. This stops your dog from learning to anticipate you removing something fun from them when you ask them to drop it.

This also acts as a double reward. Reward 1 - the treats you throw for your dog, and reward 2 - allowing your dog to have their toy back again.

Once your dog has got the hang of this, you can repeat it with a higher-value toy. Higher value toys increase your dog's arousal levels, making this exercise more difficult because they won't want to let go of the toy as readily. Arousal levels are also raised when you are playing a game of tug with your dog. So, before you ask them to Drop, let the toy go, letting it go limp to increase your dog's chance of responding successfully.

Step 4

Next, you need to repeat the game but this time, use food as the item you want your dog to drop. Choose something large and not hugely valuable to start with, like a loaf of bread, a whole carrot, a large rawhide bone, etc.

When your dog has the food item in their mouth, give the Drop cue, throw treats on the ground and push them closer to your dog's mouth with your hand.

Then, give your dog the release cue to allow them to go back to the so-so treat as an extra reward.

Once your dog does this reliably, slowly increase the value of the food on the floor. But remember always to make sure your super treat is of higher value than whatever it is on the ground.

Now, practice this as much as possible! Generalize it in different situations, with different foods to really cement your dog's learning and understanding of the Drop cue.

What Could Go Wrong?

Here are some areas where you may run into problems, and some solutions to help you overcome them:

Problem:

You have to remove whatever your dog has dropped from their mouth in a real-life scenario because it could be dangerous for them. This can make your dog more cautious about dropping things in the future, if they think you will take it away completely.

Solution:

If you need to use the Drop cue in real life, you have no choice but to remove what your dog has dropped for their own safety. However, once you have done this, you should set up some controlled training scenarios where your dog can be released back to the so-so treat on the floor. This helps to restore their trust that not everything will be removed from them totally when they drop it.

Problem:

You don't have any super treats with you when you need to ask your dog to Drop something, or the treats are of lower value than whatever they have picked up.

Solution:

If you have a toy, you could use this as a reward when your dog responds to your Drop cue. Instead of throwing treats, play a game of tug with your dog or throw the toy for them to fetch as a reward instead.

Or, if your treats are of lower value than the food they have picked up, increase the quantity of treats you give to your dog. So, instead of throwing 3 or 4 small pieces to them, throw several or give them larger pieces to increase the value of it.

Conclusion

Although we have now reached the end of the book, this is just the beginning of your training journey! And, although it may seem overwhelming to start with, with lots of commitment and dedication, you are sure to achieve fantastic results. Taking each step at a time and progressing at your dog's pace through the stages of training is the best way to achieve your goals. This training protocol will soon become part of your daily life and routine and will be something you do automatically without having to think about it too closely. Because this protocol doesn't try and eliminate your dog's scavenging entirely, it is much more natural for them to be successful and, in turn, make better progress.

Although your dog will always have the desire and need to scavenge, hopefully, you will now realize:

How to teach emergency cues to help keep your dog safe in real-life scenarios.

- How playing the core games included in this protocol can successfully manage your dog's scavenging behavior without intimidation, force or pain.
- How to provide your dog with suitable outlets for their scavenging desires in a safe environment.

- The reasons behind your dog wanting to scavenge so much and how to use this information to manage their behavior more successfully.
- The areas where you may experience potential problems and how to overcome them.
- You have the ability and knowledge to manage your dog's scavenging in a safe way.

Using the techniques you have learned from this book will help you manage your dog's scavenging and strengthen the bond and understanding you share with each other. It will help you stop viewing their behavior as something that needs to be eradicated and, instead, consider it an opportunity to understand how you can better help your dog.

So, what are you waiting for? Start putting your new-found knowledge into practice with your dog right away. And before long, you too will feel the sense of relief you have been craving, because you know your dog will be safe and able to enjoy their life as freely as possible!

Acknowledgements

It takes a village to write a book!

This book would not have been possible without the help of these amazing people:

- Charlotte Garner - Canine Author, who turned my training instructions into beautiful words and gave the text a good polish. Charlotte is a proficient author, freelance writer and blogger. Visit her website https://charlotte-garner.com/
- The amazingly talented Päivi Kokko for the wonderful sketches. Visit her website https://www.fitnsniff.fi/
- Sonja Rupp, for the lovely photos of my dogs.
- Fee Ketelsen, marketing and coaching expert who helped take my project to a whole new level
- Lisa Lang and her model Emmi with guardian Brigitte Seehuus for the amazing cover photo.
- Claire Staines and the whole Lothlorien Team for your ongoing support and for making me feel close to you, even though I'm actually quite far away.

A Special Thank You To:

I want to mention at least some of the colleagues that paved the way for force-free, science-based training protocols that I refer to in this training program:

- Dr. Ute Blaschke Berthold, a visionary trainer, and behaviorist.

- Sonja Meiburg and her fabulous book "Anti-Giftköder-Training: Übungsprogramm für Staubsauger-Hunde
- Lara Steinhoff and Sandra Bruns: „Vorsicht, Giftig! Anti-Giftköder-Training für Hunde".

The biggest thank you is to my husband Kai for his ongoing support, his patience, and for always listening to me going on about dogs and training.

Last but not least, this book is dedicated to my dogs Malinka, Nanook, and Isla, my best teachers and closest companions.

About the Author

Simone Mueller, MA is a certified dog trainer and dog behavior consultant (ATN) from Germany.

She specializes in force-free anti-predation training and is the author of the Predation Substitute Training series: "Hunting Together", "Rocket Recall" and "Don't Eat That".

Simone is proud to be an Associate Trainer at the Scotland-based Lothlorien Dog Training Club (AT-LDTC) and a member of The Initiative of Forcree Dog Training, the Pet Professional Guild (PPG) and the Pet Dog Trainers of Europe (PDTE).

Follow Simone's work on Facebook and Instagram: #predationsubstitutetraining

Learn more: http://www.predation-substitute-training.com

Simone with Nanook and Isla

About The Co-Author

Charlotte Garner is a freelance writer and author from Staffordshire, UK. She is obsessed with all things dog and can usually be found reading and researching anything dog related! She is passionate about improving the human-canine bond to help dogs become happier and is particularly interested in proving that you can use positive training methods to teach your dog anything! She currently shares her life with her 3 rescued Border Collies; Tizzy, Inka, and Delta, who have all taught her their own lessons along the way!

Take a look at Charlotte's website www.charlotte-garner.com to find out more about her work or to enquire about her writing something for you!

Charlotte with Sky, Inka, Tizzy and Delta

One Final Note

If, after reading and following this training program you feel like Don't Eat That will never work for your dog, write me an email! Yes, I'm entirely serious - humans need to learn and adapt just as much as their canine companions, and your take on the results will help me refine my approach(es) for the future.

If, on the other hand, you liked this training program and think that this is a game-changer in the relationship with your dog, please let the world know by leaving a rating and review on Amazon!

I ask this because reviews are the lifeblood of any independent book on Amazon. Without stars and reviews, there's a better-than-average chance you wouldn't have found this training program in the first place. Please take thirty seconds of your time (or potentially even less than that!) to support me as an independent author by leaving a rating.

If you would click five stars after the last page on your Kindle device or leave a positive review on Amazon through your previous orders in your account settings, I would deeply appreciate it.

Click Account & Lists in the upper right corner -> Your Account -> Orders -> scroll down your orders and then click the Write a Product Review button on the right.

It's a bit hidden, but by doing this, your review will be a "Verified Purchase", and this carries far more weight.

After all, a quick rating or review helps me to provide my dogs with more toys and treats and honestly, which dog in the world doesn't deserve more toys and treats?

Thank you very much!
Best wishes for you and your dog
Simone

Download Your Free "Don't Eat That" Training Plan

To download the training log to the Core Games as a free, printable PDF from my website, follow the link or scan the QR code:

https:// predation-substitute-training.com/ donteatthattraininglog

Glossary Of Terms

Here is an explanation of the most common terms and phrases you will see throughout the book:

Aversives – Anything that inflicts pain, fear, stress, anxiety, or makes your dog feel intimidated. This can be the use of aversive tools (i.e. shock collars, prong collars, etc.) or through the training methods you use (i.e. alpha rolling, hitting, or shouting at your dog)

Clicker – A clicker is a device that makes a 'click' noise when you press it. It's used in dog training to mark the exact moment that your dog is showing a behavior that you would like to reward and see more of.

Core Games – These are the central games that form the basis of our training protocol.

Cues – Used to explain the word you use to ask your dog to do something. A friendlier version of giving your dog a 'command' which suggests they don't have a choice.

Emergency Cue – A cue used in an emergency situation to keep your dog safe. I.e. 'drop it,' to get your dog to drop any food they have picked up from the floor.

Force-Free - Refers to not using force in any part of your dog's training or day-to-day life. I.e., not using any aversive techniques or tools.

Games - These are fun training activities you play with your dog. Because they are fun for your dog, they are much easier to incorporate into your daily routine than more formal training exercises.

Generalization - Generalization training aims to make sure your dog recognizes and understands what they've learned enough to apply it in different scenarios. To do this, you repeat their training in as many different situations and settings as you can, so your dog is comfortable doing it effectively, no matter what's going on around them. It is often the hardest part of the training, and a lot of time and effort should go into this stage to ensure the best results. Also known as 'proofing' a behavior.

Mark/Marker Word/Marking - A marker is a predictable word or noise used to tell the dog they have done something right! Some people use this in place of a clicker, but the basis of how they are used and how they work is the same. Usually 'Yes' or 'Good.' It is used to mark the exact moment that your dog is showing a behavior that you would like to reward and see more of. A marker does not get your dog to do anything, it simply lets them know this behavior is going to be rewarded.

Reinforcers - Rewards given to your dog to reinforce their behavior. This could be food, toys, verbal praise, physical affection, or anything else your dog finds rewarding.

Scavenge/Scavenging - Refers to your dog searching for discarded food, animal faeces, dead animals, or even rubbish to eat.

So-So Treats - Treats that your dog is interested in but doesn't go crazy over.

Super Treats - Treats your dog goes wild for! They should be super exciting and the best thing your dog can imagine! Super treats are reserved especially for training and excellent behavior.

The Parts of the Predation Substitute Training Puzzle

ROCKET RECALL

FOR DOGS WHO LOVE TO CHASE

FOR DOGS WHO LOVE TO SCAVENGE

HUNTING TOGETHER

DON'T EAT THAT!

If your dog loves to scavenge, you have chosen a great place to start by reading Don't Eat That! The information found here is one part of the holistic approach that forms Predation Substitute Training (PST). Understanding and implementing the entire Predation Substitute Training protocol will help you achieve better, longer-lasting results. The next on your PST training journey is 'Rocket Recall.'

What is a "Rocket Recall?"

Imagine your dog is running at full speed towards something suspicious on the ground or towards a busy road. You need something that is guaranteed to get them to turn around and run towards you and away from danger instead.

All dogs need a reliable recall, it's an essential life skill and perhaps the most important thing you can teach your dog. Having a great recall helps to give your dog more freedom and keeps them safe in the process.

You will learn how to successfully navigate scenarios like these by teaching your dog their very own Rocket Recall. Just think how great it will feel when your dog runs happily back to you when you call them, instead of you chasing after them while they ignore you completely!

And, because I know how important it is that you know how to teach a fantastic recall to your dog, this is why I have dedicated a whole book solely to helping you achieve this with your dog.

'Rocket Recall' is part of my Predation Substitute Training series of books but also works independently for many other situations.

Would you like a reading sample?

Then turn the page and learn more about the how to teach your dog a Rocket Recall!

Rocket Recall

Why Do So Many Dog Owners Struggle With Their Dog's Recall?

A reliable recall is one of the greatest challenges for many dog owners. But why is that so?

First of all, we need to understand that a recall is something aversive – negative – that is happening to the dog. It's something that goes against what they actually want to do in the moment. When we use a recall, we're asking them to turn away and abandon something that they are interested in, or something they want to check out.

Turning away from that interesting smell, person, animal, or other distraction and having to come back to us is the first "disappointment" for the dog. We naturally try to "make up" for this disappointment by giving them a treat, but often, the treat is not really a reward for our dog. Why is this? It's because the treat doesn't fulfill a need that they feel at that moment. Giving a treat is not functional – it's not part of an understood system driven by their instincts – and it can become a second "disappointment" during the recall.

Let's look at it another way, for clarity. Think back and remember the way you felt as a child when a parent called you inside for dinner, but the other kids you were with kept on playing. While you likely enjoyed eating as a normal activity, in this situation, it wasn't what you actually wanted to do. You wanted to remain playing with your friends! You may have even perceived it as a kind of punishment, as you had to leave your friends behind. You felt disappointed, sad, maybe even angry that you had to abandon what you wanted to do, even though it was for something else that you typically enjoyed.

A dog that turns away from chasing a cat, or playing with another dog, might feel the same way, even if we offer them a treat. Even though your dog loves to eat at home and in a non-distracting environment, they might not perceive that same treat as a reward when outside the home. Believe it or not, this is one of the reasons why so many dogs are hesitant or even resistant to taking treats outside.

Exploring the idea of "disappointments" within a recall further, some dog owners struggle with their dog's recall because they consciously or unconsciously punish their dog for coming back. This may look like:

- A prior loss of temper and subsequent yelling at a "naughty" dog that slipped his lead or got out.
- A waver or hardness to your voice, born out of fear that he won't come back the last few steps or may dart into the road.
- Your body language and stance changing to a threatening one when you're preparing to chase your dog down as they turn away.

Even if you don't remember doing any of these things exactly, human nature dictates you're likely guilty of at least one at some point. It was when this happened that your dog may have started to associate your recall with something negative or punitive – the "disappointment." You recalled your dog from something interesting, put them on lead, or called them away from their friends and ended the fun. According to learning theory, this is punishment.

A final familiar reason why dogs struggle to come back is a lack of training. They may understand what a recall is functionally, in the moment, but not that recall means recall regardless of the situation. Their owners have trained their recall at home, or in a similar non-distracting environment, but neglected to instill proper generalisation of the cue. In order to generalise the cue properly, you'll need to repeat it hundreds, even thousands, of times in various situations and alongside different distractions.

In order to set our dogs up for success we need to carefully structure these situations and scaffold the distractions, allowing us to work through them in a kind of "bucket list" for our dogs. In this holistic training program, we will tackle all three of the common issues that cause dog owners to struggle with their dog's recall: the reluctance to abandon something interesting, a feeling of punishment, and a lack of training. We'll also learn how to make a reward functional, ensuring it has the intended effect on your dog and doesn't feel like a disappointment.

Throughout this training, you will play games with your dog that rewire their brain, ensuring that coming back to you is no longer a punishment. Once you've properly implemented these techniques, in fact, they'll actually feel the desire to come back to you. We'll also work together to create a well-structured and scaffolded bucket list of distractions, situations and reward options to work through. Let's get started!

Rocket Recall by Simone Mueller is available as e-book, paperback (ISBN 9978-3982187815) and hardcover (ISBN 979-8753195760).

Does your dog love chasing wildlife?

If you have a dog who loves to chase wildlife and you want to learn how to manage this successfully without using force or aversive methods. 'Hunting Together' is full of useful information about how to keep your dog safe by stopping them from chasing uncontrollably. As you will discover, this is done by providing your dog with suitable and safe hunting outlets and by tapping into their natural desire to cooperate with you as a reliable "hunting partner". Instead of trying to eliminate predatory behaviour entirely, this approach provides you with much more sustainable results and at the same time it grows the relationship with your dog to a whole new level.

Are you curious why dogs love to hunt so much?
Here's a reading sample!

Hunting Together

Harnessing Predatory Chasing in Family Dogs

Why is predation such a tough nut to crack?

First of all, for our dogs' ancestors, predation was the only means of survival. Even though our dogs are typically given their bowl of food twice a day, their genes still drive them to hunt for survival. This behaviour is an intrinsic motivator that we have no control over, just like our own needs for water, food and safety.

This also leads to the second reason why the behaviour is so persistent: predation is genetically anchored: it won't go away. Your dog will not grow out of it when he matures nor can it be fixed by simply spaying or neutering your dog. Genetically-anchored behaviour is super-strong and very hard to interrupt; getting rid of it isn't an option, but guiding it is.

Predation is perfected through learning and experience. Our dogs become more successful at predation through rehearsal. With that in mind, does that mean that they should never have the opportunity to perform predatory behaviour? The answer is both yes and no. Yes, they should be prevented from doing so solo while they're out and about with you, but they should also be allowed to perform safe parts of predation in a controlled, safe environment. All the rigid prevention in the world won't stop your dog from practising predation, anyway: it's such a deeply-rooted behaviour that it can never be "switched off" entirely.

Performing predatory behaviour is an intrinsic need and motivator that our dogs have, regardless of age or breed. Problem-solving, foraging, and hunting-related behaviours are hard-wired to a part of our dog's brain that neuroscientist and psychobiologist Jaak Panksepp called the SEEKING-System. SEEKING is a core emotional system that helps our dogs find resources. If we do not offer our dogs acceptable SEEKING opportunities, they are likely to engage in unwanted behaviours instead.

Some dogs feel this need to hunt stronger than others and completely suppressing it is like pressing a lid down on a pot of boiling water: it only increases the pressure. These dogs will find an outlet for this pressure, either by going hunting alone or by developing an outlet in other areas, such as chasing bikes, stalking the cat, or destroying the sofa.

This happens because, as an intrinsic motivator, predation feels good! Hormones, such as dopamine and adrenaline, are released into the dog's body that have the same effect as drugs. To put it bluntly, predation makes our dogs high. Even though wolves take up a large number of failed chases, they continue at the behaviour for this very reason. Ignoring predation will not make it go away!

It's important to remember that the predatory sequence is triggered by visual, auditory and olfactory stimuli in a dog's environment. All our dog's senses are involved in this super intense experience, and this fact can later be used to your advantage.

What is Predation Substitute Training?

The term "Predation Substitute Training" (PST) has a double meaning. It implies that, through playing Predation Substitute Games with your dog, you'll be able to redirect predatory urges into a harmless owner-centric game, ensuring that predatory energy is released in a safe and controlled way.

The real game-changer, however, is in the deeper meaning of the term. Predation Substitute Training equips you with Predation Substitute Tools. Instead of interrupting your dog's predatory behaviour and ending the fun, you train your dog to perform a safe part to the predatory sequence instead of an unsafe part. E.g. instead of letting him chase, you let him stalk wildlife. This will still let him do what he wants to do. In short, hunt!

I have been successfully using this protocol for several years now. Nanook, my 10-year-old Australian Shepherd, used to be a big chaser. Through PST, he has become a passionate visual stalker. Rather than physically taking chase, he's now able to happily sit down and visually follow a running deer in the field while staying by my side.

While it's worked out very well for both my own dogs and my clients' dogs, I want to stress something important before we get too deep into practice and theory.

Predation Substitute Training is not a quick fix that will stop your dog from chasing. Like most proven dog training techniques, it's hard work and will require a lot of effort to put into your everyday walks to introduce and reinforce concepts. That being said, the positive outcomes that grow from this fair, motivation-centred and need-oriented training are amazing. Once PST has been successfully implemented, your dog will be more controllable in the presence of wildlife. They will be more likely to react to your recall, sharing the joy of performing safe parts of the predatory sequence with you.

Make no mistake about it: predation is pure happiness for our dogs! Imagine using that feeling of pleasure, fulfilment and motivation that our dogs find in predation to enforce useful training and deepen your bond with your dog. It's not only possible, it's a smart move!

In this training program, you'll find all of the training techniques and tools that you'll need to successfully harness your dog's predatory instincts - all without using intimidation, pain or fear:

- You will understand what predation is and why your dog loves hunting so much.
- You will have Predation Substitute Tools at hand to functionally reinforce your dog, allowing them to stop and control themselves instead of chasing after game.
- You will be equipped with several need-oriented Predation Substitute Games to create a safe outlet for your dog's predatory energy.
- And you will be provided with a safety net to interrupt unwanted predatory chasing with an emergency cue.

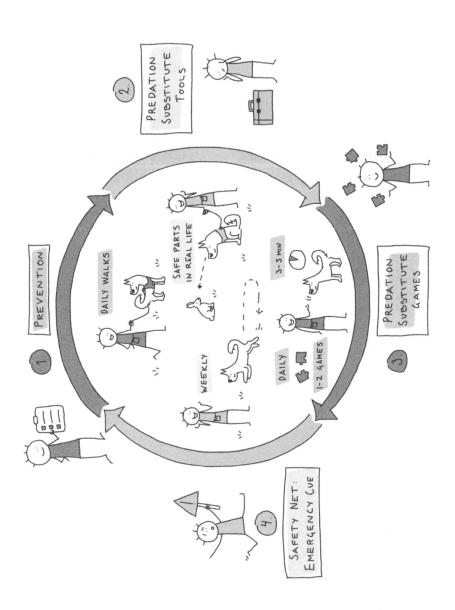

All I ask from you is that you keep an open mind while learning this motivation-centred, science-based approach, and (of course) that you have fun with your dog.

So grab your treat pouch, stuff it with delicious dog treats, and dig out your dog's most exciting toys. It's time to get started!

Hunting Together – Harnessing Predatory Chasing in Family Dogs is available as ebook, paperback (ISBN 978-3-9821878-6-0) and hardcover (ISBN 978-3-9821878-0-8)

Adding enrichment activities to your dog's life can not only help with scavenging, but with many other "problem behaviours". In "Esssential Enrichment", my co-author Charlotte Garner explores the benefits of enrichment on your dog's wellbeing. So, if you want to help your dog to be as happy and fulfilled as possible, this is the book for you!

Here's an extract to get you started:

Essential Enrichment

Here are some of the benefits of canine enrichment:

Enrichment Utilises The Natural Canine Predatory Sequence

Now, although this may sound a little bit scientific, it still applies to your dog, no matter what breed they are. Regardless of what they were bred to do, every dog naturally displays aspects of the predatory sequence. Our dog's wild ancestors relied upon the predatory sequence to find, catch, and kill prey which they ate to survive. And, although our dogs no longer need to do this so they can eat, they still retain certain parts of this natural predatory sequence. It looks a little something like this:

Orient > Eye > Stalk > Chase > Grab-Bite > Kill-Bite > Dissect > Consume

The vast majority of dogs no longer display this sequence in full, and some breeds naturally prioritise different aspects of this sequence.

For example, my Border Collies, and other herding breeds, concentrate on the *Orient > Eye > Stalk > Chase* part of the sequence, as this is what a shepherd would need them to do to round up livestock successfully. Terriers would concentrate on the *Chase > Grab-Bite > Kill-Bite* aspects of the sequence which is what makes them excellent at catching and killing rodents for pest control. And, although most domesticated dogs no longer need to carry out the dissection and consumption parts of this sequence in order to survive, it is still a natural behaviour which is deeply ingrained for them, and these aspects are something they would still likely enjoy today. This is why many dogs enjoy shredding activities like ripping open a wrapped present to access treats inside. This replicates the dissection and consumption part of the predatory sequence.

Recognising and understanding which parts of the predatory sequence apply to your dog, can help you to decide which enrichment activities would be best suited to them.

Enrichment Provides An Outlet For Your Dog's Needs

Dogs that do not have a suitable outlet to channel their natural canine behaviours can be more likely to exhibit numerous behavioural issues including; unwanted chewing of furniture and possessions, digging up the garden or flooring in the home, separation anxiety, or excessive barking, for example. This is not done because your dog is intentionally being naughty, stubborn, or badly behaved.

These less-than-desirable behaviours are happening because your dog is trying their best to meet their needs and desires in the best way that they can, in the environment they find themselves in. Pair this with potentially heightened stress levels, an excessive amount of energy, and a build-up of frustration, and it's not hard to see why your dog may be behaving in this way. So, of course, it's not a long-term solution to let your dog raid the bins, destroy your home, and continue doing things that are likely to put them at risk. Instead, if your dog is behaving in this way, use it as an opportunity to recognise that their needs are not being met to a good enough standard and to change that.

The great news is that regular enrichment activities can help your dog to combat these feelings and provide them with an outlet for their intrinsic needs. Win, win!

Enrichment Strengthens The Bond You Share With Your Dog

Not only does enrichment give your dog's brain a great deal of mental stimulation, but it can also further strengthen the bond you share with each other. Treat enrichment as an adventure of finding out what new things you could try together today; this will really get your creativity flowing. This teamwork helps build trust between you and your dog and gives your dog more confidence in you. So, if they run into a difficult situation in the future, they can be more likely to come to you for help and support. If your dog is struggling to complete an enrichment activity, feel free to help and guide them. If they are finding it difficult to find the treats in a snuffle mat, try pointing them out for them. Or, if they are unsure about what to do when you give them a wrapped present, help them by starting to unwrap the present and encouraging them to do the same. This will increase your dog's trust in you, and they will enjoy sharing an enriching experience and natural behaviours with their human.

Enrichment Helps To Combat Over-Arousal

Arousal in canine behaviour terms refers to your dog being in a heightened emotional state. It means they are showing an intense reaction or emotion to something they are experiencing in their environment. Some dogs become over-aroused very quickly, which can be hard for owners to manage. And, if a dog spends a large portion of their life in a state of heightened arousal, this is not good for their long-term health and well-being. Different dogs can experience an increase in arousal levels for different reasons. Some may experience this when they see another dog and they become excited and frustrated because they want to go and greet them. Others can experience it when they are playing high-intensity, repetitive games like fetch, because their adrenaline levels are raised.

Generally speaking, a highly aroused dog will appear outwardly over-excited and may ignore any cues or requests from their owners. This can quickly get frustrating for owners who are left feeling like they have no control over their dog's behaviour. So, instead of trying to regain control and place limitations on your dog, by using enrichment, you can provide them with an alternative outlet for these feelings. This can help your dog to calm down faster, and in turn, be in a better headspace for responding to your cues.

Essential Enrichment by Charlotte Garner is available as e-book and paperback (ISBN 978-1739395407).

Made in United States
Orlando, FL
20 September 2024

51734881R00104